JEANETTE MacDONALD

JEANETTE MacDONALD

**by
LEE EDWARD STERN**

An Illustrated History of the Movies

General Editor: **Ted Sennett**

A HARVEST/HBJ BOOK

For Phyllis, who has just succumbed to the charm of Jeanette MacDonald, and for my parents, who saw Rose Marie *five times*

**JEANETTE MacDONALD
An Illustrated History of the Movies**

Copyright © 1977 by Jove Publications, Inc.

All rights reserved. No part of this publication may be reproduced or transmitted in any form or by any means, electronic or mechanical, including photocopy, recording, or any information storage and retrieval system, without permission in writing from the publisher.

First Harvest/HBJ edition published October 1977

ISBN 0-15-646215-X

Library of Congress Catalog Card Number 77-76449

Printed in the United States of America

Stern, Lee Edward.
  Jeanette MacDonald.

  (An Illustrated history of movies)   (Harvest/HBJ book)
  Bibliography: p.
  Includes index.
  1. MacDonald, Jeanette, 1907-1965.   2. Singers—
United States—Biography.   3. Moving-pictures, Musical—
Pictorial works.   I. Title.
ML420.M135S7   791.43´028´0924   (B)   77-76449
ISBN 0-15-646215-X

JOVE PUBLICATIONS, INC.
(Harcourt Brace Jovanovich)
757 Third Avenue, New York, N.Y. 10017

Layout and Design by ANTHONY BASILE

ACKNOWLEDGMENTS

My thanks to the New York Library and Museum of the Performing Arts, *Variety*, *The New York Times*, and Charles Silver and his staff at the Museum of Modern Art, for being what they are; and to Ted Sennett, for his patience, knowledge, and expert guidance.

Special thanks to my favorite researcher and movie companion and severest critic, Phyllis Stern.

Photographs: Jerry Vermilye, The Memory Shop, Movie Star News, and the companies that produced and distributed the films of Jeanette MacDonald

CONTENTS

Introduction: Faulty Memories 11
The Stagestruck MacDonalds 17
Jeanette on Broadway 21
Jeanette and Maurice 30
Jeanette and Nelson 80
Aftermath 139
Bibliography 149
The Films of Jeanette MacDonald 151
Index 155

SAN FRANCISCO (1936). As Mary Blake

Time has not been kind to Jeanette MacDonald. Few moviegoers under fifty remember her special blend of beauty, charm, and vivacity. Even those over fifty tend to recall only her light, effortless singing and her relatively brief movie partnership with baritone Nelson Eddy. During a remarkably durable career, Jeanette made only eight films with the likeable but limited Mr. Eddy, yet the two are inseparably connected in the public mind. True, Jeanette and Nelson were the second most popular team in the whole panoply of movie musicals (topped only by Fred Astaire and Ginger Rogers), but the beguiling redhead shared some of her best vehicles with other partners. Maurice Chevalier, Allan Jones, even John Barrymore, Clark Gable, and Spencer Tracy—the determined soprano known in Hollywood as the "Iron Butterfly" more than held her own with the best male talent available.

Those from the ages of, say, thirty-five to fifty frequently have fond recollections of pleasant hours spent in the company of Jeanette MacDonald when they were quite young, but they, like their elders, usually have faulty memories. Comedians and impressionists in this age group, notably Carol Burnett, reinforce the popular misconceptions by spoofing the nose-to-nose bellowing of such easily parodied tunes as "Indian Love Call"

INTRODUCTION: FAULTY MEMORIES

and "Ah, Sweet Mystery of Life," under the mistaken impression that the enormous devotion of the MacDonald-Eddy fans in the thirties was based solely on precisely such vocal confrontations.

For those under thirty-five, except for a few discerning cinemaniacs with a taste for talent and a sense of historical perspective, Jeanette MacDonald is virtually unknown. At best, hers is a name from the far-distant past, when tastes were simple and audiences easy to please.

The real Jeanette MacDonald was a fascinating performer, literally unique in her combination of innocence and sophistication, earnestness and winning frivolity. Her physical beauty alone was extraordinary. Her features were almost *too* regular, and, in spite of her repeated admissions to being a "priss and prude," she obviously delighted in showing off her well-proportioned body and shapely legs, particularly in the delightful thirties films directed by Ernst Lubitsch, the undisputed master of "naughty" boudoir comedies. Jeanette was Lubitsch's favorite leading lady. It's easy to see why.

Of course, she could sing. Her voice was light, well-controlled, yet big enough to fill a gigantic concert hall without having to resort to microphones or amplifiers.

She sang beautifully, and was an excellent actress when given half a chance (which didn't happen often enough). She was a charming comedienne who could handle a quip or a double-take with the best of her contemporaries. She could even dance gracefully. In short, she was a pro.

The proof exists, preserved on celluloid for all to see. Naturally, in a career which included nearly thirty films and stretched for twenty years, there were bound to be a number of disappointments along the way. Many of the MacDonald vehicles could vanish without a trace and even her most ardent admirers wouldn't shed a single tear. But those that were good were very, very good, and a handful—*The Merry Widow, The Firefly, Rose Marie, Maytime*, and parts of *San Francisco*—deserve to be ranked as classics.

Like her career, the private life of Jeanette MacDonald is thought of as smooth, uneventful, and even downright dull. There is a grain of truth in this. She was successful while still very young—first on Broadway, then in Hollywood. She was married to only one man, Gene Raymond, and her marriage lasted twenty-seven years, until her death. (Her last words, murmured to Raymond on her deathbed, were, "I love you.")

But her life and career couldn't have been quite as tranquil as they appeared on the surface. Even a genial entertainer like Gene Raymond couldn't have enjoyed having his career so completely overshadowed by that of his wife, or being continually mistaken for Nelson Eddy when he and Jeanette appeared together in public.

Before she married Raymond in 1937, Jeanette had spent, in her own words, "days and nights" with her business manager, Robert Ritchie, who was frequently referred to in the press as her "fiancé." And Jeanette loved to tell of being romantically pursued (unsuccessfully) by many producers in New York and Hollywood, including the awesome Louis B. Mayer. She couldn't have been as naive and innocent as she claimed, although there's no reason to doubt her essential wholesomeness.

In spite of the stubbornness and good head for business that led her to become known as the Iron Butterfly, Jeanette made many friends, and most of them remained friendly for life. At her funeral service on January 18, 1965, the casket bearers included her costars Eddy, Chevalier, and Jones. Among the many mourners were literally dozens who had attended her marriage to Gene Raymond twenty-seven years earlier.

Jeanette was neither innovative nor profound. She lived most of her

MAYTIME (1937). As Marcia Mornay

Nelson and Jeanette

BROADWAY SERENADE (1939). As Mary Hale

life in Hollywood, and fitted easily into its social and political activities. She was genuinely at home with the tinsel beneath the tinsel that is part of life in that peculiar part of the world.

Her funeral, at the fabled Forest Lawn Memorial Park, was entirely appropriate. Although fewer than 300 were invited, an estimated 6,000 people showed up to congregate around the Church of the Recessional. Jeanette lay in a half-open casket, covered with a blanket of pink roses. Hundreds of floral arrangements overflowed the church. Among them was a huge cross of white chrysanthemums and roses from Mr. and Mrs. Dwight D. Eisenhower. Senator Barry Goldwater (a World War II buddy of Raymond) was one of the casket bearers. Before and after the service, songs associated with Jeanette, including "Ah, Sweet Mystery of Life" and "Ave Maria," were piped through loudspeakers.

Another old friend, Lloyd Nolan, delivered the eulogy. He asked a pertinent question: "There were other voices—other lovely faces. What was different about Jeanette?"

His answer was, "It was her infinite capacity for love. Love for her devoted husband—love for her family and her friends. But even more, it was her love for the entire world that brought rapture to Jeanette's voice—and rapture to those who sat entranced and silent as her message of love poured forth. . . ."

It was an easy and appropriate explanation, and perhaps there is some truth to it. But the real answer to what was different about Jeanette lies in a close examination of her work.

She *was* different, that's certain. Of the dozens of Broadway and opera stars who were recruited to Hollywood in the early days of sound, only one—Jeanette MacDonald—had an enduring movie career. Fanny Brice, Sophie Tucker, Marilyn Miller, the popular Irish tenor John McCormack, and many others had brief flings on the screen. The beautiful operatic soprano Grace Moore scored a personal triumph in 1934 with *One Night of Love*, but her Hollywood career was over by 1937. Only Jeanette survived and triumphed.

Some weeks after her death, a memorial tribute in the *Chicago Daily News* said, "The older folks will mourn and remember Miss MacDonald and the young will never know what they missed."

This book is one small attempt to persuade new generations of moviegoers to understand why Jeanette was different, and to remind movie audiences of all ages of a kind of beauty, charm, and radiance sadly lacking in today's world.

THE STAGESTRUCK MacDONALDS

Jeanette Anna MacDonald was born in Philadelphia on June 10, 1903. Her grave marker contains the inscription, *Jeanette MacDonald Raymond, Beloved Wife*, and the dates 1907-1965. In typical Hollywood fashion, she had pushed her birthdate farther and farther ahead, until the year of her birth "officially" became 1907 when she signed with Paramount in 1929.

Her first recorded stage appearance was as Old Mother Hubbard in a school recital at the Philadelphia Academy of Music in 1907, when she was only four years old. Her parents, Daniel and Anna Wright MacDonald, were very proud. Although neither of the MacDonald parents had any theatrical experience, both were stagestruck, and encouraged all three of their beautiful daughters to study music, dance, and acting. MacDonald, a building contractor who dabbled in local politics, had every reason to boast about his children's achievements. Elsie, the eldest, was something of a child prodigy. She had taught herself to play the piano long before she learned to read. The second daughter, Edith Blossom (usually called Blossom), could sing and dance well, and later had a minor but successful career on stage and screen. But little Jeanette was clearly the most promising.

It was a close-knit and decidedly "square" family. The MacDonalds were devout Presbyterians. The social highlight of the week was ice cream at home every Sunday night. But regardless of the fluctuating family finances, there was always enough money for weekly lessons for all three talented daughters. It wasn't long before the MacDonald girls were well known for their appearances in amateur theatricals in Philadelphia. Elsie seemed destined to become a concert pianist, Blossom and Jeanette to make their mark on the stage.

At the age of six, Jeanette appeared in a series of "mini-operas" staged by a Philadelphia producer named James B. Littlefield and his wife, Caroline. At eleven, she spent her summer vacation touring with Al White's "Six Sunny Song Birds" in Pennsylvania and New Jersey. At twelve, she appeared in many church and amateur productions and taught Sunday School at her neighborhood Presbyterian Church.

When Jeanette was sixteen, her sister Elsie eloped with a sailor, putting an end to her budding concert career. (She was later to marry twice more.) By this time, Blossom had moved to New York, where she was dancing in a Ned Wayburn "prologue" called *The Demi-Tasse Revue*.

A fashion pose around 1930

One fine fall day, when her father went to New York on business, Jeanette played hooky from West Philadelphia High. Without their father's knowledge, Blossom had arranged an audition for her kid sister for the revue. The redhead from Philadelphia got her first Broadway job. She was in the chorus, billed as an Indian Maiden and a Twinkling Star along with many other Indian Maidens and Twinkling Stars.

With both children appearing on Broadway, the devoted MacDonalds decided to move to New York and supervise their daughters' careers. Daniel MacDonald died a few years after the move, but Anna MacDonald remained a concerned and protective stage mother for many years.

The *Demi-Tasse Revue* was a miniature stage show offered at the Capitol Theatre as a prologue to a feature-length silent film. In 1919, the Capitol and other theaters offered "complete" stage-and-screen productions for 30 cents a ticket. Jeanette, who was listed in the program as "Janette" MacDonald, stayed at the Capitol for other revues until January of the following year, when she joined the chorus of a "legitimate" Broadway musical, *The Night Boat*, with music by Jerome Kern. During its 148 performances, Jeanette progressed from chorus girl to understudy to supporting role.

Legend has it that Jeanette left *The Night Boat* before it formally closed because she was so tired of resisting the amorous advances of one of the play's backers. It was a story that was to be repeated many times about her experiences in many plays, and Jeanette herself repeated these probably true tales tirelessly.

The beautiful redhead wasn't out of work for long. Within a week, she was rehearsing for her first "solo" songs on Broadway. She took over the featured role of Eleanor Worth in "last year's hit," the durable *Irene*. After a week in New York, Jeanette went with the road company to Boston, where she was billed as a member of the Broadway cast.

The Great White Way of the early twenties was a far cry from the Broadway of today. In 1920, no fewer than 157 plays opened in New York. Many folded after only a few performances, but there was plenty of work available for promising, popular, conscientious young performers.

JEANETTE ON BROADWAY

It was also possible in 1920 to appear on Broadway and study at a local high school at the same time. Jeanette attended two New York schools, first Washington Irving, then Julia Richman High School. When she traveled to Boston with *Irene*, however, her formal schooling ended. She had just completed the tenth grade.

The studies she *really* enjoyed were her vocal lessons with a series of coaches and her dancing lessons under Albertina Rasch, who later moved to Hollywood and choreographed the dances in several MacDonald vehicles.

By the summer of 1921, Jeanette was again unemployed and making the rounds of the casting offices. She was no longer living with her parents. Her sister, Blossom, was on tour with a show, so Jeanette shared a hotel room with another young dancer. She helped to pay the bills with a number of modeling assignments, and spent much of the sweltering summer posing in fur coats.

On Broadway in BOOM! BOOM! (1929)
with Frank McIntire

In September of 1921, she joined the cast of a desert-island musical, *Tangerine*, but left a few months later when the show went on the road. Jeanette asked for an increase in salary so that she could take her mother with her. Instead, she received her walking papers.

Later that year, she landed her first leading role in a "Greenwich Village revue" called *Fantastic Fricassee*. This "Bohemian" potpourri, with skits by such free souls as Ben Hecht and Maxwell Bodenheim, was roundly panned by the critics and seemed headed for an early death until a strange set of circumstances conspired to forestall its doom. The show was to have appeared before a group of prisoners at Sing Sing, but an official of the Prison Reform Association vigorously objected to showing "these naked dancing girls" before a captive audience. Because of the resultant publicity, *Fantastic Fricasse* lasted for a respectable 112 performances.

Jeanette's big break came in 1923, when she was chosen for the ingenue lead in a musical called *The Magic Ring*, starring a fiery Hungarian performer billed as Mitzi. (Her last name was Hoag, which apparently wasn't exotic enough to be mentioned.) Others connected with the show who were later to make their mark in the movies were the portly Sydney Greenstreet and the ubiquitous costume designer Adrian. Jeanette was described in the advertisements as "the girl with gold-red hair and sea-green eyes." The critics, ecstatic about the show, singled out the young redhead for her striking appearance and effortless singing. *The New York Times* said she was "among the merits of the evening," and the critic for the then-influential *New York Tribune* called her ". . . one of the glowing things to be commemorated, like the keepsakes of which she eloquently sings."

Jeanette MacDonald had arrived as a Broadway performer. Her salary rose to more than $250 a week, a handsome sum for those times.

Jeanette stayed with *The Magic Ring* for its full run at the Liberty Theatre, and then went on tour. In all, she performed the ingenue lead more than 640 times. She was now enough of a star to warrant lengthy interviews in many papers, and to have a parade of stage-door Johnnies and other admirers vying for her favors. One of these was a young architecture student at New York University, with whom she had what she later described as her first serious romance. We "promised to be true to each other," she said, but by the time she returned to New York in 1925, the romance was over.

While Jeanette was savoring her first taste of fame, a blond, handsome young actor named Ray-

mond Guion was appearing in a Broadway play called *The Potters*. He was later to appear with Humphrey Bogart as one of the two male leads in a comedy, *The Cradle-Snatchers*, supported by those two grand old character actresses, Edna May Oliver and Mary Boland. Still later, as Gene Raymond, he was to meet, woo, and wed Jeanette MacDonald in Hollywood.

In December of 1925, Jeanette played one of the leads in the short-lived *Tip Toes*, with music and lyrics by George and Ira Gershwin. She earned $350 a week, more than enough to pay the rent on a relatively opulent apartment and support her mother comfortably.

Never "at liberty" for long, she soon became the second female lead in *Bubblin' Over*, a musical version of the perennial farce, *Brewster's Millions*. Jeanette sang four songs, including the title tune, with music by Richard Meyer and lyrics by the prolific Leo Robin. The show was successful on the road, but lasted barely a week in New York.

In mid-1926, Jeanette's sister Blossom, by now an established supporting actress, got married. Like Jeanette, she wed only once. She remained with her husband in New York and Hollywood until he died in 1960.

Jeanette's next role was in a tepid imitation of the highly successful *No, No, Nanette* called *Yes, Yes, Yvette*, put together by the same producer, H. H. Frazee, to take advantage of *Nanette*'s popularity. After more than a year on the road, *Yvette* ran for only forty performances on Broadway. Jeanette scored a personal triumph in the Midwest, but she, like the show, received only lukewarm notices in New York.

But she was now certifiably a *star*, and was treated as such by the press, the public, and producers. In 1927, the fabled Schubert brothers chose her for the starring role in a musical, *Sunny Days*, which, like so many other shows of the time, toured around the country before opening on Broadway. After the New York premiere in February, 1929, at the Imperial Theatre, Brooks Atkinson, long an admirer, wrote that the "dainty" Jeanette could "dance buoyantly and . . . sing with the best voice in the company." The show lasted for 101 performances and then toured the country again, with Jeanette still in the lead.

The Schuberts kept her busy. In 1928, while she was starring in an ill-fated vehicle called *Angela*, the then-popular screen star Richard Dix invited her to Hollywood for a screen test. She traveled to California with hope in her heart and made the test, but for the time being, nothing came of it. Meanwhile, with Atkinson and other critics still

ding her, Jeanette starred in another Schubert production, *Boom! Boom!*, which staggered through two months in New York before being shipped to Detroit and Chicago.

In Chicago, Jeanette received a telegram from the brilliant director of frothy, sophisticated silent comedies, Ernst Lubitsch. Lubitsch had seen her screen test with Fox, and thought he might consider her for the leading role in his first sound movie—but only if she could sing. He flew to Chicago and heard her in *Boom! Boom!* He made up his mind. Jeanette was to play opposite the quintessential French lover, Maurice Chevalier, already an international favorite, in Lubitsch's *The Love Parade*.

In June, 1929, when euphoric American investors were certain there could be no peak to the cascading stock prices, Jeanette packed her bags and set off for Hollywood. Since she didn't know how long her film career would last, she arranged to hold on to the lease for her New York apartment.

In 1929, when Jeanette and her ever-present mother arrived in Hollywood, the films had found their voice and were feverishly searching for profitable ways to use it. Since 1927, when *The Jazz Singer* paved the way for the integration of song and dialogue in the movies, producers had been combing the Broadway and concert stages for "names" whose voices could match their looks. In addition to the Broadway luminaries previously mentioned, opera stars Lily Pons and Lawrence Tibbett were lured away from New York by lucrative contracts, but none of these singing stars made more than a few successful films. Many "straight" actors recruited during the early thirties, on the other hand, remained to become rich and respected staples of the silver screen. Among them were Fredric March, James Cagney, Humphrey Bogart, Edward G. Robinson, Claudette Colbert, and Barbara Stanwyck, all of whom were to return to the legitimate stage only intermittently throughout their long and lustrous screen careers.

Paradoxically, even the Depression of late 1929 and the thirties did little to temper the search for new talent. While many if not most American families were having trouble paying the weekly grocery bills, moviegoing became a weekly habit and was considered one of the necessities of American life.

JEANETTE AND MAURICE

Jeanette seems hardly to have been aware of the economic crisis that was turning the country inside out. Like many of her day and her profession, she devoted herself tirelessly and singlemindedly to furthering her own career.

While Mrs. MacDonald hovered protectively around Jeanette at all times, the young actress also depended heavily for professional and personal advice on a good-looking, prosperous young stockbroker, Robert Ritchie. In New York, Ritchie had been her constant escort. In Hollywood, she telephoned him frequently for comfort and counsel.

For the moment, however, she concentrated her energies on her first screen venture, *The Love Parade*, directed by Ernst Lubitsch and costarring Maurice Chevalier. On the set, the virtually unknown soprano definitely played second fiddle to the great continental favorite, Chevalier. Lubitsch was intoxicated with Jeanette but, accustomed to the fuller-bodied heroines then so popular in his native Europe, felt she was much too thin. Jeanette recalled later that he was constantly feeding her malteds.

To today's filmgoer, *The Love Parade* seems long, dull, and primitive. Jeanette and Maurice were to

In the early thirties, at Paramount

be associated with Lubitsch's first and worst musical, just as they would be paired in his last and best, *The Merry Widow*, five years later.

The story of *The Love Parade* concerns a beautiful queen (MacDonald) in a mythical European state who is forced to choose a husband to carry on the royal line. Her choice is the dashing roué, Count Alfred (Chevalier), who is not of royal lineage but comes from "a distinguished family" (his great-grandfather was the illegitimate son of one king and his grandmother was the sweetheart of another).

At first, the count is delighted, but he soon learns that, as prince consort, he performs his only duties at night. During the day he has no tasks, no authority, nothing to do. Bored and humiliated, he draws up a plan to save the country from financial crisis, but he is ignored. To preserve his manhood, he decides to withhold his favors from the queen, and threatens to leave. By the final scene, she is begging him to come back, saying she will follow him anywhere and addressing him as "my king." Not exactly a plot to gladden the hearts of women's libbers, but certainly a serviceable-enough framework for a frivolous operetta.

The trouble is, this slight framework is virtually buried under tons of rococo scenery, clumsy sequences featuring the principals singing directly to the camera, and heavy-handed attempts at humor. The celebrated Lubitsch touch shows itself occasionally, but too often it is smothered under creaky camerawork and dismal dialogue.

The first scene is promising, a typical Lubitsch teaser. Behind the credits, a pair of hands are skimming through a French fashion magazine. We are in Paris, city of fashion, champagne, and chorus girls, all of which are shown in a beguiling montage. Lupino Lane, as Jacques, the count's valet, sings a song to "Champagne" as he sets an elegant table in an ornate hotel suite. Elsewhere in the suite, his master, the count, is confronted by a furious girl friend, who has found a garter in his room. She hikes up her skirt to show it is not hers. She pulls a gun, aims it at him, and is about to shoot when there is pounding at the door. Her husband has arrived. She shoots herself.

The husband takes the gun from her hand and aims it at the count, then pulls the trigger. There is a loud retort, but the count is unhurt. The gun has been filled with blanks.

The girl, realizing what has been going on, recovers. She and her husband prepare to leave when he notices that her dress is unhooked and awkwardly tries to fasten it. Exasperated by his clumsiness, she skips over to the count, who finishes the job instantly. After the husband and wife leave, the coun

THE LOVE PARADE (1929). As Queen Louise.
At left: Virginia Bruce

THE LOVE PARADE (1929). With Maurice Chevalier

tosses the gun and garter into a drawer well-stocked with guns and garters.

A pleasant, fast-moving scene, but the promise is never fulfilled.

Jeanette, however, is fresh and beautiful, and reveals more of her shapely legs and cuddly body than in any later film. Scenes in her boudoir and her bathtub, complete with lacy see-through lingerie and suggestive yawns and stretches, reveal the radiant redhead at her sauciest and naughtiest. Chevalier, on the other hand, overplays so much that his famous grin threatens to become a grimace.

The supporting team, the English music-hall star Lupino Lane (uncle of Ida Lupino) and the talented songstress and comedienne Lillian Roth, are appealing as comic servants, especially in a rubber-legged song-and-dance routine to "Let's Be Common," but the Victor Schertzinger score is lackluster, as is the dialogue by Guy Bolton.

The critics of the time, however, liked the film, but concentrated on Lubitsch's direction and Chevalier's acting. A few were also entranced by Jeanette. The durable Richard Watts wrote in the *Herald*

THE LOVE PARADE (1929). With Maurice Chevalier

Tribune that her performance was "entirely winning." He felt that nothing she had done on Broadway could compare with her sparkling screen debut. "Blessed with a fine voice, a sense of comedy and a definite screen personality, she registers an individual success that makes her future in the new medium an enviable one," he said prophetically. *The New York Times* critic, Mordaunt Hall, thought she sang "charmingly" but wrote disparagingly of her "speaking," although he admitted "... it was quite evident that the fault lay with the treacherous microphone and not with Miss MacDonald's diction."

Chevalier was nominated for a 1929 Academy Award for his work in *The Love Parade* and another Paramount film, *The Big Pond*, co-starring Claudette Colbert, but lost out to George Arliss as Disraeli.

When *The Love Parade* was completed, Paramount sent Jeanette back to New York for the premiere and a series of promotional appearances. Her mother, of course, accompanied her, and Ritchie was again her constant companion. She spent some of her time in the East making her first professional recordings, a lucrative sideline she was to continue for more than thirty years. She was soon summoned back to California by Paramount, which was about to produce a movie version of the popular operetta *The Vagabond King*, starring the handsome, popular Broadway star Dennis King. It was to be the first of five ill-fated pictures starring Jeanette in 1930.

The ads for *The Vagabond King* understandably emphasized the stirring Rudolf Friml melodies and the equally stirring voice of Dennis King. They played up "... the thundering throb of 'Song of the Vagabonds' in the glorious golden voice of Dennis King," the "gorgeous Technicolor," and the "thrills and adventure, excitement, romance." King and MacDonald were called "Broadway's favorite romantic stars."

Lillian Roth again appeared in a supporting role, as did Warner Oland, who was later to become the best-known of Hollywood's several non-Oriental Charlie Chans.

(A nonmusical version of this romantic tale of the dashing fifteenth-century rogue-poet, François Villon, titled *If I Were King*, scored a tremendous success in 1938, with Ronald Colman as Villon.)

The blame for this ponderous 1930 version of a tuneful stage musical appears to be equally divided between the director, the German-born Ludwig Berger, and the male star, who was unable to adapt his larger-than-life stage style to the dissimilar demands of the screen. Jeanette had no opportunities to display her wit, and stood stock still

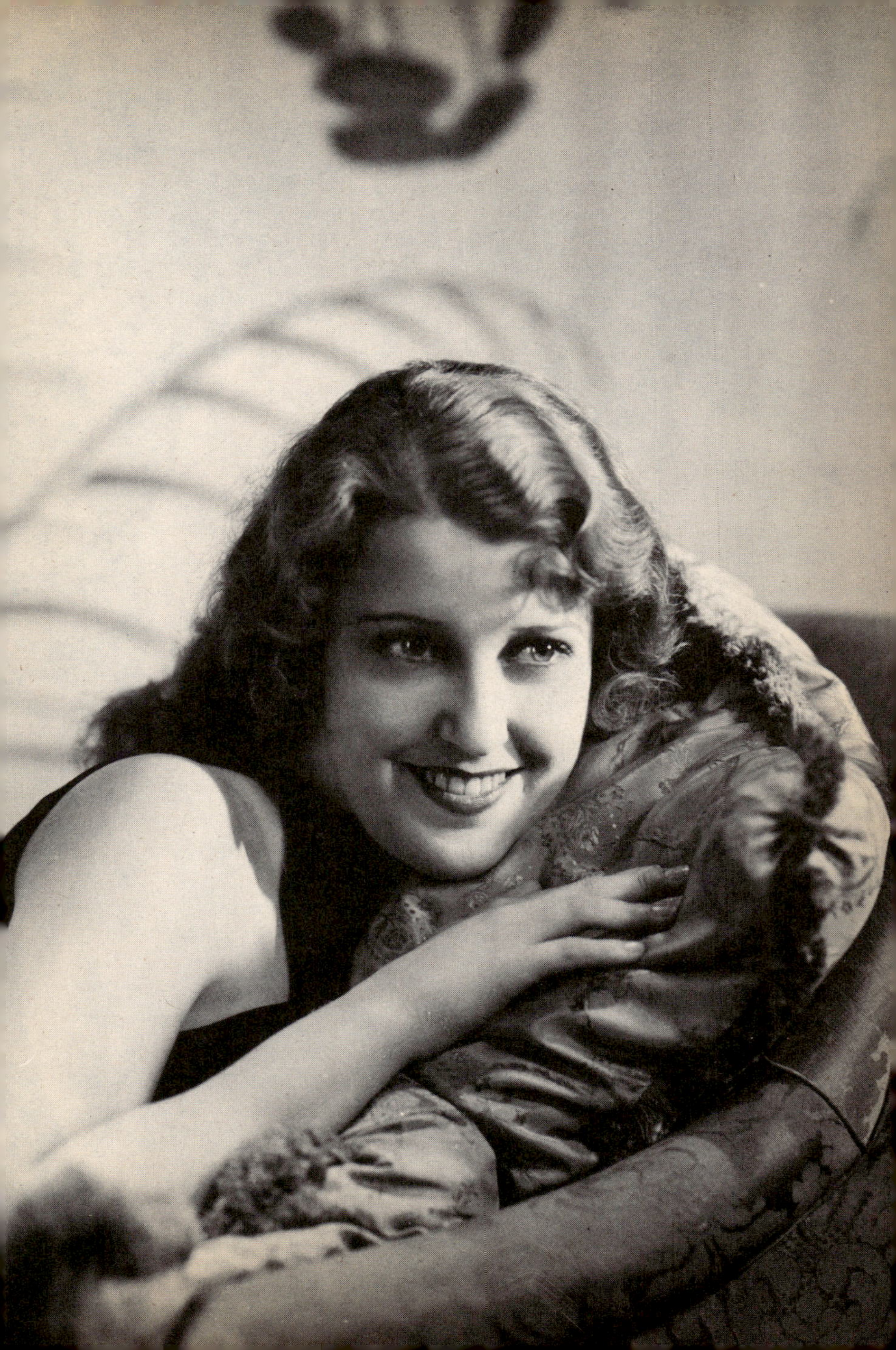

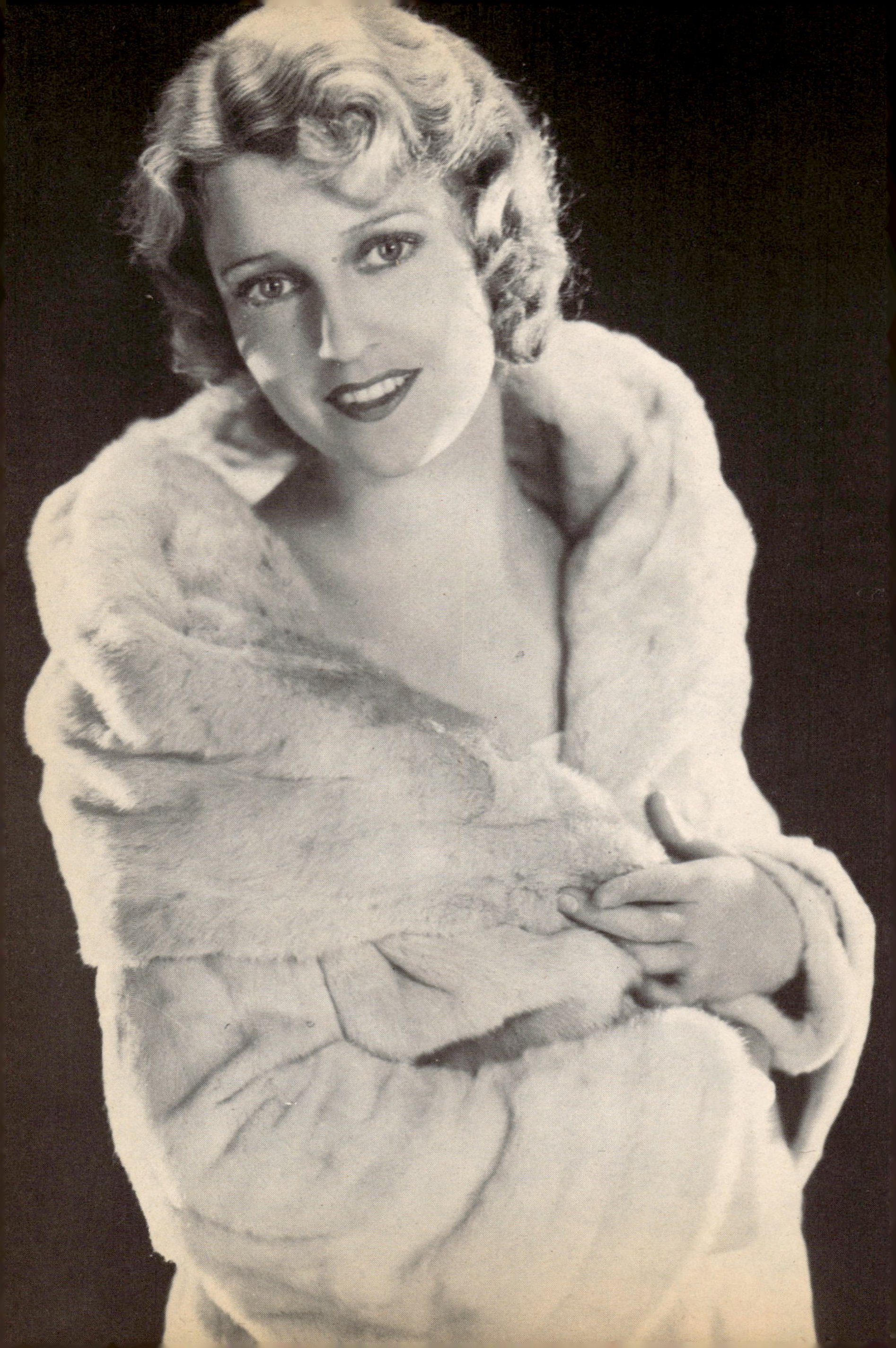

THE VAGABOND KING (1930). With Dennis King

most of the time while delivering her lines or songs. In later years, she was to refer to the film scornfully, and loved to tell about her biggest number, in which she sang the beautiful "Only a Rose." King was miffed that he, too, wasn't included in the scene, so shadows and awkward portions of his anatomy, including his nose, keep appearing in inappropriate moments. Jeanette called it the "only a nose" sequence.

The major critics disliked the film as much as Jeanette did. Only Mildred Martin of the *Philadelphia Inquirer* dissented, finding *The Vagabond King* "the most successful film operetta to be made so far." The *Times* critic called the movie "beautiful and often stirring" but again criticized Jeanette's diction: "Her enunciation never gives the slightest indication of belonging to the period."

In spite of *The Vagabond King*'s generally unfavorable reviews, Jeanette was considered a saleable commodity, and received a bid from United Artists to sign a contract for at least one film, with the possibility of more to come. Since she had no business manager at the time, she wired to New York to ask

THE VAGABOND KING (1930). With Dennis King

Robert Ritchie to join her in Hollywood as her business adviser. As a result of his first visit to the West Coast, in 1930, Ritchie remained to become Jeanette's full-time manager, and later to represent other Hollywood stars as well.

Jeanette had meanwhile filmed a routine to a song called "Sweeping the Clouds Away" for an all-star revue called *Paramount on Parade*, in which many of the stars of that studio, including Chevalier, Richard Arlen, Jean Arthur, Gary Cooper, Fredric March, and William Powell, had brief turns before the Technicolor cameras. Although both Jeanette's and Chevalier's sequences were directed by Lubitsch, the studio was apparently disappointed with her performance. The sequence was eliminated from the English-language version but inexplicably retained for the Spanish-language version, *Galas de la Paramount*. In that version, she also appeared as a Spanish-speaking mistress of ceremonies, acting as a "pointer" for the various acts.

For her second Paramount picture in 1930, Jeanette was reunited with Lubitsch for *Monte Carlo*, a somewhat sprightlier film than the previous year's *The Love Parade*, but one still marred by clumsy camerawork and, in addition, hampered by the vacuity of its leading man.

As "insurance" for the success of the film, Paramount had imported the somewhat fey English song-and-dance man, Jack Buchanan. Buchanan, with his silly grin and lifted eyebrows, was a pleasant enough performer who would be perfectly at home in a Noël Coward comedy. In *Monte Carlo*, however, he comes off as only slightly less precious than his silly-ass screen rival, the amusing Claude Allister. As in *The Love Parade*, there are a few scintillating scenes. In one, Count Rudolph, the hero, explains his system at the gaming tables. If he happens to be standing near a brunette, he bets on red. If he's near a redhead, he bets on black. What if he's standing near a blonde? "I ask her where she lives."

There is one truly memorable sequence in which Jeanette sings the haunting "Beyond the Blue Horizon" as she leans out a train window, her fluffy scarf billowing in the wind. The sounds of the locomotive provide the underlying rhythm, while a group of unlikely farmhands interrupt their work in the fields to listen and wave.

Jeanette's final film for Paramount before departing for United Artists was *Let's Go Native*, a musical directed by Leo McCarey and starring Jack Oakie as a chauffeur with the unlikely name of Voltaire McGinnis who is shipwrecked on an island ruled by a Brooklyn sailor (Skeets Gallagher). Jeanette is a ship's passenger who

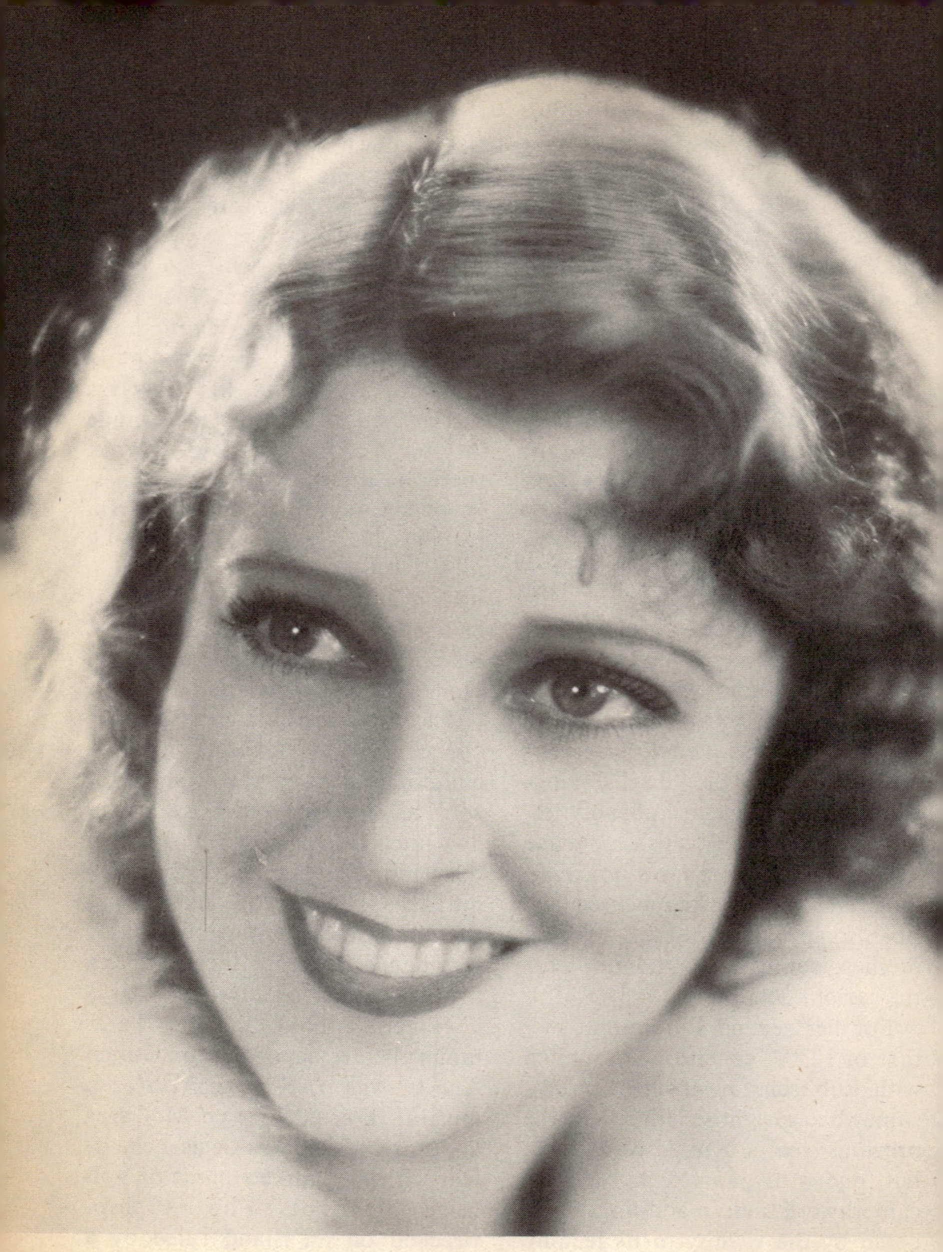

becomes romantically involved with the sailor. McCarey was still not quite comfortable with sound, after having directed some excellent silent comedies. (Three years later, he was to guide the hilarious comedy classic, *Duck Soup*, with the Marx Brothers.) *The New York Times* called this slight effort a "ludicrous hodgepodge." Jeanette agreed.

Her only United Artists film was heartily condemned by the critics and shunned by the public. *The Lottery Bride* is worth noting only because, for the first time, Jeanette MacDonald was *the* star, billed above her costars, John Garrick, Joe E. Brown, and ZaSu Pitts (who had survived the transition to sound by transforming herself from an ingenue to a comedienne, playing up her wispy, fluttery voice). Although *The Lottery Bride* contains the first original score for the movies by the operetta king, Rudolf Friml, the songs were apparently a curious combination of rejects and fragments excavated from drawers and wastebaskets for the occasion. *Variety* thought "there isn't a worthwhile performance in the entire cast" and warned theater-owners not to book this turkey. Jeanette fared poorly as a Norwegian girl who enters herself in a wife lottery and, after some foolish complications, wins her boyfriend after all.

MONTE CARLO (1930). With Jack Buchanan

Jeanette's reputation had been firmly implanted, but she had made only two worthwhile movies, both of them with Lubitsch. As consolation, however, she made her radio debut on NBC, and her pure voice and pleasant personality led to requests that would keep her busy in that popular medium for many years.

By December of 1930, studios and audiences alike had tired of the tedious parade of assembly-line movie musicals, exemplified by *The Lottery Bride*. The figures tell the story. The studios had churned out more than sixty musical films in 1929, and about seventy-five in 1930. In 1931, only a handful were produced. Jeanette had embarked on a three-picture deal with Fox, negotiated by Ritchie. The first of the three, *Oh, For a Man*, costarring Reginald Denny, had already been completed when the studio decided to eliminate the majority of the musical sequences. For a plot which centers around two singers, the great opera star Carlotta Manson (Jeanette) and a burglar who aspires to become a professional singer (Denny), this was a mistake.

Still, there are some good moments. For the first time, Jeanette sings a full-fledged aria (from *Tristan and Isolde*) on the screen. The movie opens with her on stage, singing. When the curtain comes down to thunderous applause, she does her hilarious parody of a pampered prima donna (later to be echoed in the exquisite opening scene of *Rose Marie*). She takes her curtain calls shyly and graciously, but between curtsies she maliciously berates the tenor, the management, and "that son of an electrician." After that frothy opening, the film goes downhill fast, as Carlotta reforms her burglar boyfriend. Once they are married, he objects to being known only as the husband of a prima donna (shades of *The Love Parade*). The only saving grace is Jeanette's unexcelled comic talent.

Her two remaining Fox films, *Don't Bet on Women* and *Annabelle's Affairs*, both released in 1931, were out-and-out drawing-room comedies, devoid of music. *Don't Bet on Women* was a pleasant and modest film, directed stylishly by William K. Howard, and featuring a cast of gifted farceurs, including Edmund Lowe, Roland Young, and Una Merkel. Its lightweight plot centered on a wager between Lowe and Young which involves Young's flirtatious wife (Jeanette). *Variety* called it "an inept story, superlatively acted." Jeanette, Una Merkel, and Roland Young were universally praised, and the film was successful at the box office.

The last of Jeanette's Fox films, *Annabelle's Affairs*, was adapted from a successful 1918 play by Clare Kummer, *Good Gracious*

MONTE CARLO (1930). As Countess Vera von Conti

Annabelle. It costarred Victor McLaglen, and featured the ubiquitous Roland Young. McLaglen is a gruff but kindly Montana miner who marries the spoiled Jeanette after she is thrown from her horse and forced to spend the night in his cabin. Figuring she has been "compromised," he makes an honest woman of her. Jeanette is amused, but finds that the marriage is binding. She leaves him, but his checks keep coming.

Years later, Annabelle is living luxuriously in New York when her husband shows up again. He is now rich and polished. After many complications, they find they truly love each other, and there is the traditional happy ending.

Many of the mostly favorable reviews commented with relish on Jeanette's then-obligatory scenes in lacy lingerie. In fact, the anonymous reviewer for *Time* magazine, which had ignored the actress in *The Love Parade*, was surprised and delighted at her comic talents, noting that previously she had been known chiefly for "an aptitude for undressing before the camera quickly and almost completely with becoming grace and without embarrassment."

While her screen career was proceeding slowly but steadily, Jeanette was worrying about other problems. For no apparent reason other than rumors about her immorality, the loquaciously moral Miss Mac-

LET'S GO NATIVE (1930). With James Hall

THE LOTTERY BRIDE (1930). With ZaSu Pitts and Joe E. Brown

Donald's pictures had been banned in parts of Europe. After the release of *Monte Carlo*, which had been filmed entirely in Hollywood, Crown Prince Humbert of Italy (a "certain crown prince," as Jeanette later called him) was said to have been caught in a clandestine love affair with "a blonde girl." Many Europeans, fed by sensational newspaper reports, leaped to the conclusion that the "blonde girl" was Jeanette, who was and always had been a redhead. Then, when she made three nonsinging films in a row, rumormongers in Europe spread the incredible story that Jeanette had been shot by the crown prince's wife and that her twin sister had replaced her on the screen!

To disprove all this nonsense, Jeanette decided to make her first trip to Europe for a concert tour. Thousands of curious Frenchmen awaited her arrival in Le Havre. According to her own account, the tumultuous crowds caused her to lose her mother, her secretary, Robert Ritchie, and one shoe "between the boat and my car."

When Jeanette arrived in Paris from Le Havre in September of 1931, the crowds that gathered to greet and cheer her were said to be the largest since the arrival of Charles Lindbergh four years earlier. Her run at the Empire Theatre was an unalloyed success, and Jeanette became the toast of Paris. When Maurice Chevalier attended one performance and rushed to the stage for a kiss and an embrace, the press immediately decided the two were having an affair.

(In reality, although Jeanette and Maurice respected each other's talents, they were wary of each other's ambitions. Chevalier thought Jeanette had no sense of humor, and was visibly annoyed when she objected to his telling what he called "a risqué story" on the set. Jeanette, for her part, thought Chevalier crude and pushy. Ritchie, meanwhile, had been making *his* influence very much felt, and Chevalier spoke scathingly of Jeanette's and Ritchie's "marriage, or arrangement." Whether true or not, Chevalier later said that Ritchie would frequently arrive on a set, throw a temper tantrum, and reduce Jeanette to tears, after which, "when it was time to film a scene, she was ready to work, all smiles.")

In public and in private, Jeanette and Maurice were polite and cordial to each other, but they were certainly not close friends. The European press wasn't bothered by the facts. From their reports, it seemed that she was carrying on simultaneous affairs with a titled European, Chevalier, and Ritchie. Jeanette had really arrived. Like it or not, she was saddled with a reputation as an international temptress.

From Paris, she flew to London, where she repeated her triumphant recitals. The audiences were wildly enthusiastic about her potpourri of operatic arias, popular tunes, and songs associated with her films. The affable Jack Buchanan, who had enjoyed working with Jeanette in Hollywood, threw a glittering party for her, attended by most of the English social set of the day. Jeanette was kept happily busy with recitals, parties, and recordings. She was certifiably an international star of stage, screen, radio, and recordings.

While in Europe, she received many stage and film offers, including a tempting invitation from a French producer to perform the title role in *The Merry Widow*, the most popular operetta in history. Ritchie, however, advised her to return to Hollywood for a new two-picture deal with Paramount.

The first of these was to be an altered version of a Lubitsch silent hit, *The Marriage Circle*, with Jeanette and Maurice guided by a new director, the talented George Cukor. Cukor started on the film, now retitled *One Hour With You*, in 1932, but decided to leave after only a few weeks of shooting. He liked Jeanette but couldn't get along with Chevalier, and felt that "the Lubitsch touch" was needed for this frivolous nonsense about a jealous wife (Jeanette) who wins back her wandering husband (Maurice) by showing that she, too, can play the game of flirtation and assignation. Lubitsch, who was busy with a serious antiwar film called *The Man I Killed*, was called in to save the new musical, but devoted only part of his time to it. As released, *One Hour With You* contains some scenes directed by Cukor, some by Lubitsch. Nobody seems to know precisely which is which. The credits list both directors, although B.P. Schulberg, head of Paramount at the time, had disliked Cukor's work and wanted to remove his name.

In spite of these problems and complications, *One Hour With You* was warmly received by the critics. Regardless of their differences in attitude and personality, or perhaps *because* of them, Jeanette and Maurice always played well together. Surprisingly, Lubitsch received the lion's share of the praise, with Chevalier a close second. *The New York Times* thought Jeanette was "fair and graceful," but most of its review was devoted to the assumed director and the breezy male star.

For her next, and ultimately her last, Paramount film, Jeanette was again paired with Chevalier in an original and innovative musical

THE LOTTERY BRIDE (1930). Leading a musical number

OH, FOR A MAN (1930). With Reginald Denny

directed by Rouben Mamoulian, *Love Me Tonight*. Back in 1929, Mamoulian had been responsible for a nearly forgotten musical classic, *Applause*, with Helen Morgan. In this, his first sound film, Mamoulian had brilliantly captured the seamy world of burlesque, concentrating on a fading stripper who, after a tawdry and heartbreaking career, finally commits suicide. In its harsh and candid look at backstage life, *Applause* was well ahead of its time, and suffered the box-office neglect predicted for it by the Paramount bosses.

Now, in 1932, Mamoulian was as uncompromising as ever. He had just completed *Dr. Jekyll and Mr. Hyde*, which was to win an Academy Award for Fredric March. When Adolph Zukor approached the successful director "with tears in his eyes," as Mamoulian later recalled the incident, and asked him to produce and direct a film starring box-office favorites Chevalier and MacDonald, he agreed reluctantly. But the movie was to be made under conditions stipulated by Mamoulian.

DON'T BET ON WOMEN (1931). With Edmund Lowe and Roland Young

DON'T BET ON WOMEN (1931). With Una Merkel and Roland Young

Mamoulian set to work putting the elements of the film together. First, he purchased a two-page outline of "a kind of fairy tale" from a European writer named Leopold Marchand. Next, he imported Richard Rodgers and Lorenz Hart from Broadway to write the clever, mocking music and lyrics.

Under Mamoulian's tutelage, as he himself put it, "all the songs were carefully planned, with the lyrics to advance the story line, and their place in the story itself designed before the writers of the screenplay were engaged."

What emerged was a new kind of movie musical, with songs seamlessly integrated into the somewhat absurd plot. The story concerns the mythical Princess Jeanette, doomed to die unmarried because nobody in her realm is her social equal (except for an 85-year-old man and a boy who "will be 12 on his next birthday"). Chevalier plays Maurice, a high-society tailor who is becoming impoverished because his aristocratic clients don't pay their bills. (It was common in the early thirties for certain approachable stars to retain their first names for fictional roles. Al Jolson, Eddie Cantor, and Jack Benny were frequently known as Al, Eddie, and Jack in their screen vehicles.)

To woo the princess he loves, the tailor pretends to be a baron, and attends a costume ball in his own clothes, which are mistaken for an "Apache" costume. The supposed baron advises Jeanette that her riding habit is helplessly out of date. While redoing her outfit, he is caught with the lovely, half-dressed princess. To extricate himself from this compromising situation, he vows he'll create an entire new outfit for her. He does so, and reveals himself as a tailor.

Exposed, the jaunty tailor is forced to leave the country on a train. Jeanette, propelled by her passion for him, follows on horseback, but she can't get the engineer to stop the speeding locomotive, so she gallops on ahead. In a strikingly dramatic scene, she stands on the tracks, hands on hips, facing the onrushing engine. Brakes screeching, the train stops within inches of her. Maurice rushes out and swoops her up in his arms. They embrace in a cloud of steam. In spite of the differences in their social standing, they will presumably live happily ever after. After all, this is a fairy tale.

Helping the action along is a string of lilting tunes, including "Lover," "Isn't It Romantic," and "Mimi," the jaunty ditty that was to become a Chevalier trademark. Supporting roles were handled ably by such dependable troupers as Myrna Loy, C. Aubrey Smith, and the eternally bemused Charles Butterworth.

The film was profitable for the financially ailing Paramount, and most of the critics were favorably impressed. A few, however, complained that the film lacked the light and lively Lubitsch touch, and Mildred Martin of the *Philadelphia Inquirer* thought it "uninspired," in spite of the Rodgers and Hart score. Present-day audiences are likely to agree with this assessment. *Love Me Tonight* now seems a mildly amusing film with some cleverly satirical scenes and a wealth of memorable melodies.

Mamoulian and Rodgers got along so well together that, eleven years later, Rodgers and his new collaborator, Oscar Hammerstein, chose the director of *Love Me Tonight* for their historic stage musical, *Oklahoma!*, which paved the way for a new generation of smoothly integrated Broadway musicals. (Mamoulian also directed such Broadway classics as *Porgy and Bess* and *Carousel*.)

During the shooting of *Love Me Tonight*, Robert Ritchie had been more evident than ever. Mamoulian, a stern disciplinarian, ordered Ritchie barred from the set. Chevalier was overjoyed, Jeanette chagrined. She was apparently beginning to realize that the former stockbroker was not exactly furthering her career.

In December, 1932, Jeanette, with no more pictures under contract, set off on another concert tour of Europe. She played to cheering audiences in France, Belgium, Switzerland, Holland, and Spain, and bought a villa in the south of France, partially paid for by the then-enormous salary of $13,000 a week she received for her personal appearances.

While Jeanette and Ritchie were in Europe, Irving Thalberg, the "boy wonder" of Metro-Goldwyn-Mayer, was making plans to lure the radiant redhead to his studio. He was positive that 1933 would see renewed interest in musical films, and wanted Jeanette as his lead entry in the coming race for studio supremacy.

With Ritchie's help, Jeanette signed a contract with MGM, but didn't return to the United States for almost a year, after considering and rejecting a number of offers to sing with European opera companies.

Thalberg, who had reached a compromise with Louis B. Mayer and started his own production unit under the MGM banner, proved to be a good prophet. After lying dormant for a few years, the movie musical was essentially rejuvenated in 1933 and 1934. Jeanette played a vital role in this revival, but there were many other notable contributors, particularly Busby Berkeley, with his panoramic and kaleidoscopic choreography; the unbeatable musical team of Fred Astaire and Ginger Rogers; and the quintessential movie moppet and box-office darling of the decade,

ANNABELLE'S AFFAIRS (1931). With Victor McLaglen

ANNABELLE'S AFFAIRS (1931). With Victor McLaglen and Roland Young

curly-haired Shirley Temple.

By the time Jeanette returned to the film capital, Louis B. Mayer had taken a personal interest in her career. However, neither he nor Thalberg came up with a suitable property to show off the talents of their new acquisition, so Ritchie negotiated with United Artists for a projected musical, *The Duchess of Delmonico's*, which was to have costarred Herbert Marshall. For some reason, the film was never made.

Thalberg had wanted Jeanette to star in *I Married an Angel*, with a script by Moss Hart and a score by Rodgers and Hart, but the idea was shelved because Mayer was obsessed with making wholesome "family pictures," and *Angel* was a risqué story about an angel who loses her wings on her wedding night. (It was made into a Broadway musical in 1938 and became Jeanette's and Nelson Eddy's last picture together in 1942.)

Finally, almost in desperation, Jeanette agreed to costar with fading silent-screen star Ramon

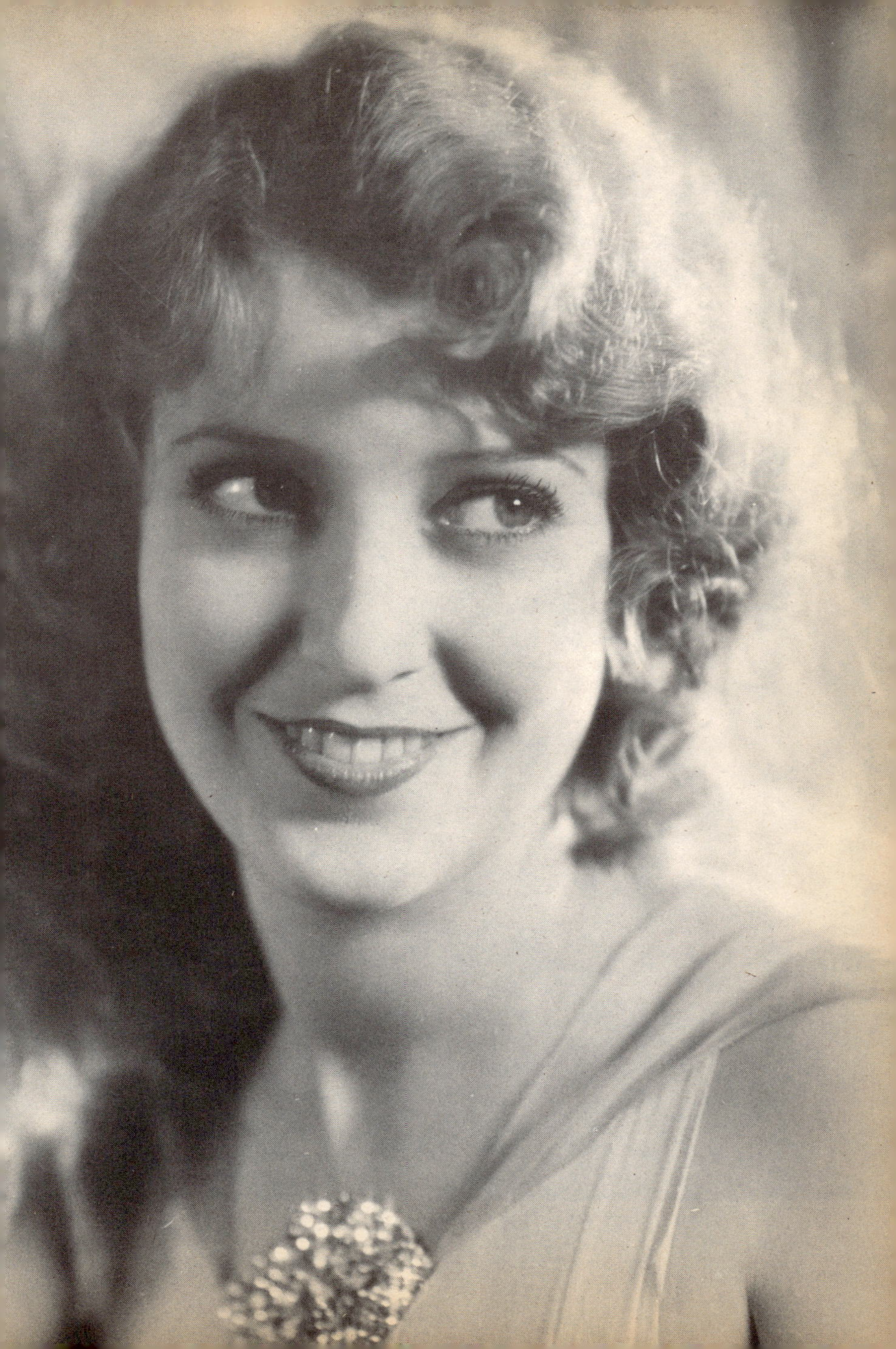

ONE HOUR WITH YOU (1932). With Maurice Chevalier

Novarro in a Hollywood version of the Broadway hit *The Cat and the Fiddle*, with music by Jerome Kern and lyrics by Otto Harbach. (The black-and-white picture contained one "three-color Technicolor" sequence, the show-within-a-show that constitutes its finale.)

Novarro was still mildly popular with screen audiences, but the peak of his fame had been reached when he played the title role in the epic silent film, *Ben-Hur*, which also featured the handsome, bushy-browed Francis X. Bushman as the magnetic villain. MGM hoped to regain some of Novarro's former box-office appeal by taking advantage of his pleasant singing voice, pairing him with the increasingly popular Jeanette, and playing up the melodic tunes of Jerome Kern, including "The Night Was Made for Love," "She Didn't Say Yes," and "Poor Pierrot." Unfortunately, the director, William K. Howard, who had worked with Jeanette on *Don't Bet on Women*, was far more interested in heavy-breathing dramatic films than light, frothy comedies.

The Cat and the Fiddle is about a music student who falls in love with a budding composer, and then rushes in at the last minute to play the lead in his show and "save" it. This old story obviously required fast movement and snappy dialogue to make it bearable, but Howard, saddled with a pedestrian

ONE HOUR WITH YOU (1932). With Maurice Chevalier

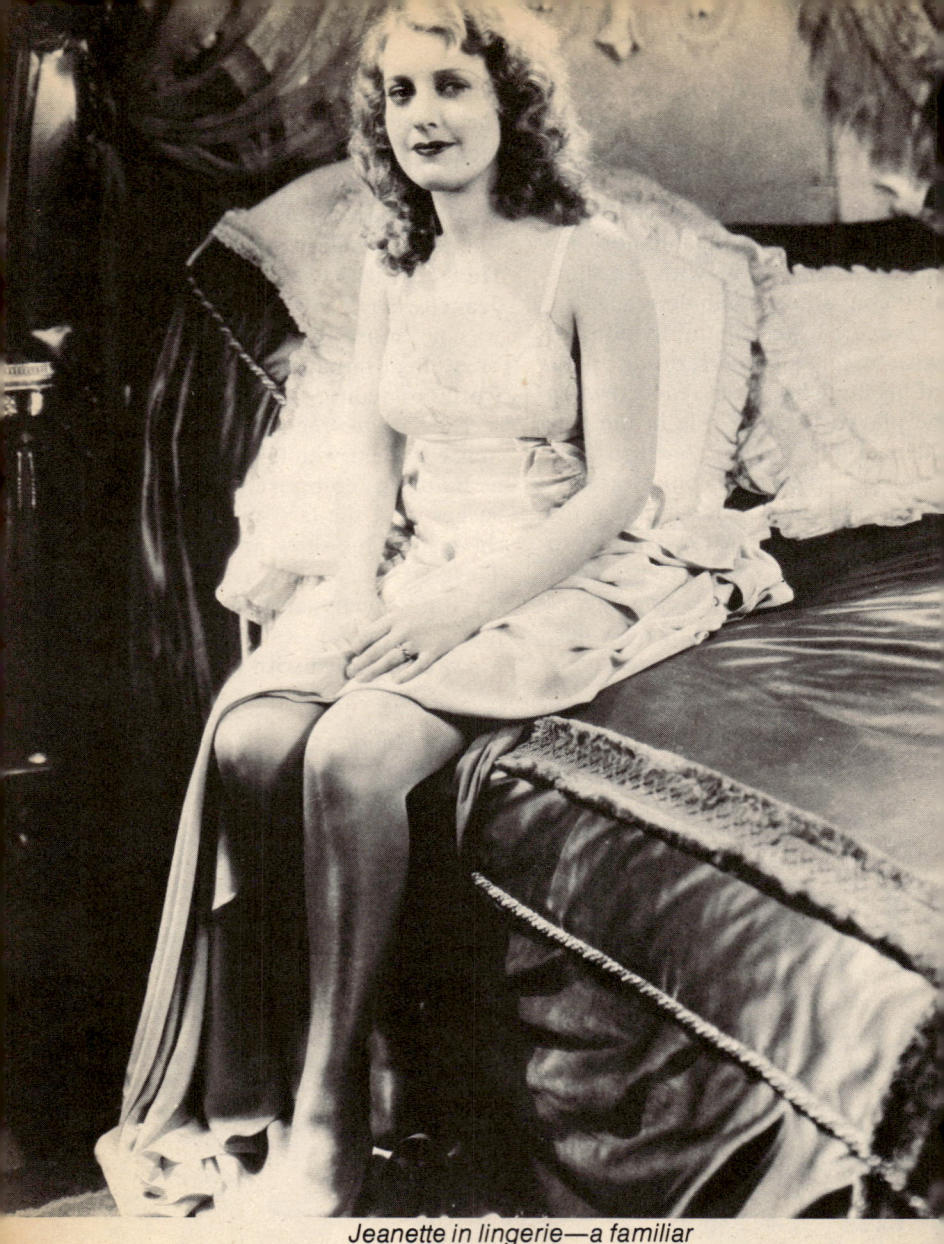

Jeanette in lingerie—a familiar pose of the early thirties

creenplay, never managed to achieve more than a pale imitation of Lubitsch's naturally graceful tyle.

Even so, *The Cat and the Fiddle*, aided by a light-hearted supporting cast including Frank Morgan, Charles Butterworth, Jean Hersholt, and Vivienne Segal, was a mild hit, although it didn't provide the box-office bonanza Louis B. Mayer had anticipated.

The shooting had been, as usual, marred by personality clashes. Vivienne Segal, who played Jeanette's competitor for the affections of Novarro, complained bitterly that her part had been reduced drastically on Jeanette's instructions. She later insisted that Jeanette had arrived on the set with this pleasant greeting: "Hello, Viv, have you seen your part? It stinks." She claims that this one vindictive act effectively ruined her Hollywood career.

Although *The Cat and the Fiddle* was no great triumph, it gave Jeanette one memorable moment. At its premiere in the Capitol Theatre in New York in February, 1934, Jeanette, her sister Blossom, and her mother were in the audience. The Capitol was still combining stage shows with screen presentations, and Novarro was the star of the "live" portion. Sitting in the crowded theater, looking at the same stage where she had made her first appearance on Broadway in

LOVE ME TONIGHT (1932). With Maurice Chevalier

LOVE ME TONIGHT (1932). With Maurice Chevalier and C. Aubrey Smith

The Demi-Tasse Revue, Jeanette must have realized how far she had come in fifteen years.

But her best and most glorious picture was yet to come, and she wouldn't have to wait long. *The Merry Widow*, already the most popular operetta in stage history, was about to become the single best filmed operetta in screen history.

Ever since its premiere performance in 1905, Franz Lehar's sparkling salute to gaiety and frivolity had been a worldwide success. By 1934, when MGM decided to produce the third screen version, studio publicists estimated that it had been performed in twenty-four languages and, in one unnamed year, had been seen and applauded by 18,000 audiences around the world. Even making allowances for the usual studio hyperbole, there's no denying that this fast-paced, spicy musical contained all the ingredients to account for its unequalled appeal. Its waltz theme, perhaps the most familiar waltz of all time, starts slowly and sensuously, then builds to a whirlwind climax of infectious melodic enthusiasm. And it is only one of the constant delights studding Lehar's irresistible score.

LOVE ME TONIGHT (1932). With Maurice Chevalier

Maurice Chevalier, arriving in New York on his way to Europe in 1934

A studio publicity photograph, around 1934

The movie rights to *The Merry Widow* had been sold to a French producer by Lehar and his collaborators, Victor Leon and Leo Stein, as far back as 1923. MGM had acquired the rights in 1925 for an ambitious silent version directed by Erich von Stroheim. Now, in 1934, rights were still being disputed, but MGM finally received legal permission to mount a full-blown sound version.

Once all the legal hurdles were cleared, the studio went to work planning a major feature film. MGM had previously lured Jeanette, Maurice, and Lubitsch from one of its prime competitors, Paramount, and was still trying to establish itself as *the* major outlet for big-budget pictures.

When it came to casting *The Merry Widow*, Chevalier argued for Grace Moore, the personable prima donna from the Metropolitan Opera, to play opposite him. He and Jeanette had had their tiffs in the past, and he was afraid of becoming known as part of a team, rather than a superstar who could hold his own with, or dominate, *any* leading lady.

Both Lubitsch and Irving Thalberg, however, held out for Jeanette. By this time, Lubitsch was convinced she was the perfect heroine for his type of film—bright, beautiful, beguiling, and extremely funny when given half a chance. Thalberg was initially torn between Grace Moore and Jeanette, and it might have been Miss Moore's persistent campaigning for the role that finally turned the tide against her.

In her autobiography, *You're Only Human Once*, Miss Moore unashamedly tells how she pursued Thalberg and tried to win the part. She even offered to do it for no salary. But her pleas were not heeded. As she tells it, "Finally Thalberg told me bluntly that Lubitsch didn't want me, didn't believe in me, was sold on another girl. . . . Well, they should have believed me. *The Merry Widow* was a flop."

Time has shown how wrong she was. True, *The Merry Widow* was surpassed in box-office receipts during the year of its release by Miss Moore's Columbia vehicle, *One Night of Love*, but that film pales in comparison with the bubbly, magnificently realized *Merry Widow*, one of the few screen classics that seem eternally fresh and even more entrancing with each viewing.

Everything works in this splendid movie. There's never a boring moment, never a sagging scene. The ingredients are chosen perfectly and mixed to perfection—Chevalier's swaggering, winking audacity, Lubitsch's mocking, fast-moving direction, the flavorsome new lyrics provided for the lilting Lehar melodies by Lorenz Hart and Gus Kahn. Perhaps

THE CAT AND THE FIDDLE (1934). As Shirley Sheridan

THE CAT AND THE FIDDLE (1934). With Ramon Novarro (kneeling)

the most important ingredient of all is Jeanette at her entrancing, sophisticated best.

Besides Grace Moore, many other Hollywood favorites had been considered for the role of Sonia, the wealthy widow who alone can rescue the tiny mythical country of Marshovia from imminent financial disaster. Lily Pons, Vivienne Segal (for whom getting this part would have been sweet revenge), even Joan Crawford—each had her advocates, but Lubitsch and Thalberg wisely held out for Jeanette. The part fits her like an elegant pair of fine kid gloves.

Although the plot was considerably changed from that of the familiar stage version, the basic story line remains the same. It's still a light-hearted tale about how a group of colorfully caricatured government officials conspire to convince a handsome young man to court the richest widow in their land, so that her funds will remain in the country. In the stage version, however, the gentleman in question is a prince who had jilted the widow years ago. In the Thalberg production, he is a captivating captain with a well-deserved reputation for wooing and winning any girl who happens to capture his fancy.

As the credits appear, a large magnifying glass sweeps over a map of Europe, attempting to locate the tiny Central European kingdom of Marshovia. Finally, it is found—an almost invisible dot.

The movie immediately swings into action, with Marshovian troops marching merrily though the cobblestoned streets of a typical comic-operetta kingdom, singing an entirely appropriate song, "Girls, Girls, Girls." The pace is established, and it never lets up.

The troops are led by the smiling captain whose every step brings squeals of delight and cries of "Danilo, Danilo" from the pretty young girls lining the street and waving from windows. Only one woman does not respond. It is the veiled widow Sonia, dressed in black, whose black carriage rolls through the streets oblivious to the spectacle of the resplendent soldiers marching through the sunlit streets.

The remainder of the film shows how Danilo pursues and eventually weds the beautiful widow, prodded by the king (George Barbier) and his staff, including the peerless Edward Everett Horton as the bumbling Ambassador Popoff. Along the way, there is an abundant array of intrigue and complications with accompanying opportunities for bright and brittle musical numbers.

First, Danilo sends the widow a message with his modest self-assessment: "Madame Sonia, if you ever meet Captain Danilo, let me tell you—he is terrific." He de-

With director Ernst Lubitsch and Maurice Chevalier

livers the note himself, and to his consternation soon learns that she considers him "not terrific."

But after he leaves, she finds herself thinking about the audacious stranger even while she is mourning her late husband, who is so incidental to the plot that we learn almost nothing about him. Finally, she decides to go off to Paris and discard her widow's weeds. "There's a limit to every widow," she decides. In a brief and brilliant sequence, to fitting background music, the rows of identical black dresses in her wardrobe turn to white, and even her furniture and her little lap dog turn from black to white.

Danilo is ordered by the cabinet to follow the lovely Sonia to Paris, after the king discovers the obstreperous captain in a somewhat compromising situation in the queen's boudoir. With the queen (Una Merkel) vouching for Danilo's abilities, the king realizes that the captain is just the man to lure the lonely widow back home. Danilo gaily agrees.

Ambassador Popoff (Horton), after some initial misunderstandings, acts as go-between in Paris. "Have you ever had diplomatic relations with a woman?" he asks Danilo. The captain assures the ambassador that he can handle the assignment easily, but tonight—ah! tonight belongs to the ladies of Maxim's.

Sonia, of course, also decides to go to Maxim's—incognito. She is mistaken for one of the "girls," and instructed by the manager to mingle with the customers and order as much champagne as possible.

Sonia joins Danilo at a table. He can't understand why the girl he knows as "Fifi" is initially so reluctant to go upstairs to a room with him. As she coyly resists his advances, he becomes more and more captivated by her. But he threatens to leave until Sonia dances around him, to the opening strains of the "Merry Widow Waltz;" she then sings the lyrics seductively and unforgettably. They embrace on a velvet-covered couch, Jeanette carefully remembering to keep one foot on the floor in accordance with the dictates of the Breen office, then Hollywood's keeper of moral standards.

When "Fifi" leaves the room abruptly, all the other girls rush in

THE MERRY WIDOW (1934). With Edward Everett Horton and Maurice Chevalier

THE MERRY WIDOW (1934). *As Sonia*

THE MERRY WIDOW (1934). With Maurice Chevalier

THE MERRY WIDOW (1934). With Maurice Chevalier

At Grauman's Chinese Theatre, Maurice Chevalier helps Jeanette place her footprints in cement.

and try to console the angry, frustrated Danilo. He has fallen in love with the beautiful new Maxim's girl, and feels he can't carry out the scheme to marry the widow. So he gets thoroughly drunk and Popoff has to sober him up quickly for the planned big meeting with Sonia at the embassy ball.

During the ball, the two principals, for the first time, confront each other in their true identities. Sonia taunts Danilo by telling him his beloved "Fifi" is dead, having "committed suicide by jumping into a cold bath."

He is furious but, once again, the Merry Widow waltz exerts its magic. In a scene of wondrous enchantment, Sonia and Danilo dance through room after room, first through a deserted ballroom, which suddenly becomes alive with dancing couples swirling through every doorway, then in a gorgeously mirrored hall awash with music and waltzing couples, then, again, alone together.

But when Sonia realizes that Danilo's wooing of her is only a scheme to get her money, she rejects him. He has failed, so he is sentenced to prison back in Marshovia. (Even in jail, Danilo leads a gilded life. His handcuffs are gold, and they are engraved, "Dolores to Danilo.")

After a hilarious courtroom scene, in which the widow defends him on the basis that he fulfilled his orders by lying to her and deceiving her, Danilo and Sonia are locked inside the cell together by the cabinet members. Champagne is sent in, and the cell is sprayed with perfume.

As the strains of the pervasive waltz are heard again, a minister appears at the door to the cell. Sonia and Danilo are married, and the kingdom is saved. As they kiss, the waltz rises to an ecstatic crescendo.

In spite of Grace Moore's jaundiced assessment, *The Merry Widow* was by no means a flop, but it wasn't an unalloyed success at the time of its release. *The New York Times* loved it. *Variety* thought it would be "dynamite at the box office," but it wasn't. It remained for viewers in later years to rediscover the incandescent and unequalled charm of this nearly perfect filmed operetta.

The Merry Widow was to be Lubitsch's last movie musical, Chevalier's last American picture until the fifties, and the last film to unite the peerless talents of Jeanette, Maurice, and Lubitsch. The very next year, Jeanette was to become the darling of moviegoers as a result of her pairing with the handsome baritone, Nelson Eddy. As for Chevalier, he was almost fifty, a bit long in the tooth for a romantic, rakish film idol, and it was to be thirty years before he was to score another screen success with the same

Maurice Chevalier

On the MGM lot with opera star Lily Pons

studio's delightful *Gigi*, in which he played an aging roué with the same grace and insouciance that characterized his best work as a much younger man.

It's hard to say why Jeanette and Maurice worked so well together. Offscreen, they were almost diametric opposites. Jeanette didn't drink or smoke; Maurice did both. Jeanette was proud of her control; he bragged of his passion. Jeanette called Chevalier derisively "the fastest derriere-pincher in Hollywood," and Maurice publicly took offense at her puritanical airs.

Yet, on screen, particularly under Lubitsch's guiding hand, they were an inimitable team. She could easily match his insults, winks, and insolent style. Her light operatic voice and his music-hall growl complemented each other. At their best, as in *The Merry Widow*, they fed on each other's vitality, and they provided a brand of crackling wit that neither could match with other screen partners.

After *The Merry Widow*, Jeanette never again quite recaptured the same sparkle and sophistication. She scored many other triumphs and had many other opportunities to display her charm and acting ability, but only *The Merry Widow* exhibits Jeanette MacDonald at the top of her form, with that irresistible combination of qualities never approached by any other screen performer. She was the *perfect* operetta heroine. *The Merry Widow* is lasting proof.

JEANETTE AND NELSON

By 1935, Louis B. Mayer was convinced that Jeanette would soon be a very big star, in spite of the vast amounts of money poured into *The Merry Widow* and its disappointing reception, particularly in small towns. Mayer felt the actress-singer should now be showcased in wholesome "family" pictures, made to appeal to the family trade. No more of this suggestive continental sophistication.

Jeanette at first resisted his attempts to star her in a movie version of the familiar Victor Herbert operetta, *Naughty Marietta*, but finally succumbed to the logic of his reasoning that Americans wanted simple sentimental stories with happy endings—although she never did succumb to his increasingly insistent amorous advances.

During that same year, bothered by persistent complaints about Robert Ritchie's interference with her life and his antics on the set, Jeanette severed her relationship with him. An old friend, Helen Ferguson, became her press agent and unofficial adviser. (Ritchie later became a film and television producer. He died in obscurity in New York in 1972.)

Naughty Marietta was planned as a quality film, but the budget was severely limited. The director was the competent W.S. Van Dyke II, known as "One-Shot" Van Dyke. By that time, Woody Van Dyke was famous in Hollywood for having completed the clever and successful *The Thin Man*, with William Powell and Myrna Loy, in only twelve days. He had also directed *Tarzan, The Ape Man* and an offbeat 1931 musical movie, *Cuban Love Song*, featuring Lawrence Tibbett, Jimmy Durante, Lupe Velez, and frequent renditions of that catchy little tune, "The Peanut Vendor." He was a pleasant, easy-going outdoorsman, accustomed to putting up with his stars' eccentricities and making the best of them. Van Dyke agreed with Mayer that Jeanette would be just right for the role of the Princess Maria, who escapes from the court of France disguised as a husband-seeking "casket girl" and finds true love in colonial Louisiana.

The only problem was the casting of the male lead, Captain Warrington, a rugged mercenary soldier who had to be handsome, stalwart, and a stirring singer. The Broadway singing star Allan Jones seemed to meet all these requirements, but was under contract to the Schuberts. Almost in desperation, Jeanette, Mayer, and Van Dyke finally agreed to take a chance on an obscure young contract player, Nelson Eddy.

Right from the start, Jeanette and Nelson got on well together.

NAUGHTY MARIETTA (1935). With Nelson Eddy

NAUGHTY MARIETTA (1935). With Douglass Dumbrille

Both were conscientious and hard-working. Both loved opera. They shared memories of a Philadelphia in which both had started their careers. Both were unabashedly "square." Jeanette was more than willing to overlook Eddy's inferior acting skills because she admired his big voice, pleasant personality, and good looks.

Nelson Eddy was born in Providence, Rhode Island, in 1901, but moved to Philadelphia when he was fourteen, after his parents separated. Forced to quit school to help support his mother, he held a variety of jobs while still in his teens, among them stints as a telephone operator and mailroom clerk. At sixteen, he lied about his age and experience and became a reporter for the *Philadelphia Evening Bulletin*, where he covered trials, politics, and sports. In spite of his lack of formal education, he was bright and well-read. At nineteen, he became an advertising copywriter. All this time, he was studying voice, at first intermittently, then with the idea of becoming a professional singer.

In 1921, at the age of twenty, Eddy received his first check for singing—$25 for entertaining at a private club. The following year, he appeared in a musical called *The Marriage Tax* at the Philadelphia Academy of Music. (One of his fellow performers was Max de Schauensee, later to become a

Nelson Eddy

NAUGHTY MARIETTA (1935). With Nelson Eddy

prominent music critic known nationally for his appearances on the radio broadcasts of the Metropolitan Opera.)

By this time, young Nelson had decided to devote himself singlemindedly to a singing career. He appeared in several Gilbert and Sullivan productions in the Philadelphia area, and in 1924 won first prize in a music contest, enabling him to appear as Amonasro in *Aida* with the Philadelphia Opera Society at the Academy of Music. The *Philadelphia Record* called his first appearance in opera "electrifying," and said that he looked like "a star from the moment he appeared on stage." That same year, he traveled to New York to appear at the Metropolitan Opera House as Tonio the clown in a Philadelphia Civic Opera Company production of *Il Pagliacci*. By 1928, when he was put under contract by Columbia Concerts, he had appeared in major roles in twenty-eight operas.

Nelson Eddy's voice became familiar on radio broadcasts as far back as 1932. (In 1936, his frequent renditions of "Shortnin' Bread" on the Edgar Bergen–Charlie McCarthy show made him a nationwide target for affectionate parodies.)

Eddy was a very promising artist with a vibrant if somewhat limited voice, and was even considered capable of standing in for the great soprano Lotte Lehman when she became ill and was unable to fulfill a recital engagement. That was in 1933 in Los Angeles. In the receptive audience that night was Ida Koverman, assistant to Louis B. Mayer. She raved about the young singer to the boss, and suggested he'd do well in the movies.

Her enthusiasm wasn't surprising. With his reddish hair flecked with gray and white strands (although he was usually referred to as blond), his erect posture, and his pleasant, regular features, Eddy stirred the hearts of many female admirers. It was said that when he made the rounds of booking offices, all typing ceased. He was uncommonly handsome.

Mayer tempted the young concert artist to emigrate to Hollywood. He offered a lucrative 28-week contract with a 7-year renewal option. The money was irresistible for a man who had been accustomed to scrambling for a living, and whose previous ambition had been to make $10,000 a year singing.

Before *Naughty Marietta*, Eddy had made three brief appearances in other MGM films. In *Broadway to Hollywood* (1933), starring Alice Brady and Frank Morgan, he sang one song in a vaudeville number. Later that year, in *Dancing Lady*, which starred Joan Crawford and Clark Gable and was notable for a clog dance expertly executed by

Fred Astaire, Eddy appeared as "himself," singing a Rodgers and Hart tune, "That's the Rhythm of the Day." In 1934 he appeared in one production number in a minor film, *Student Tour*, starring Jimmy Durante and Charles Butterworth. He was hardly earning his salary.

But now, after more than once deciding that he had been foolish to give up his promising concert career for the movies, Eddy was being costarred in an ambitious if small-scale version of an operetta that had been a staple of American road companies since 1910. Nelson was nervous and unsure of himself, not without reason. Jeanette and Van Dyke tried hard to make him relax, but he still seemed stolid if not wooden. To make Eddy feel more at home, his private singing teacher, Edouard Lippe, was brought in and given a small role, which he performed very well. At one point, the usually placid Van Dyke is said to have screamed, "I've handled Indians, African natives, South Sea islanders, rhinos, pygmies, and Eskimos and made them act—but not Nelson Eddy."

Naughty Marietta was an enormous success, although it seems long and static today. Audiences loved, and went home humming, the old familiar favorite "Italian Street Song," the rousing "Tramp Tramp Tramp," and especially, "Ah, Sweet Mystery of Life." To its eternal credit, the movie never takes itself seriously. Frank Morgan and Elsa Lanchester are amusing foils as the governor of New Orleans and his understandably suspicious wife. Other effective bits are contributed by Douglass Dumbrille and Akim Tamiroff. Jeanette manages to preserve a certain twinkling, tongue-in-cheek attitude throughout, but Eddy often looks a little awkward and uncomfortable.

The audiences of the time obviously didn't notice, or didn't care. At the Capitol Theatre in New York, where Jeanette had made her first Broadway appearance, *Naughty Marietta* had a record-breaking run.

Ed Sullivan, the widely read columnist of the *New York Daily News*, called Jeanette and Nelson "the new team sensation of the industry." He was right. *Naughty Marietta* went on to become one of the 100 top-grossing films of all time. Audiences all over the country saw the movie, and liked what they saw. They clamored for more of the same, and MGM was happy to oblige.

Naughty Marietta was a landmark film for Jeanette MacDonald, not because it was such a good movie—in retrospect, it wasn't—but because it paved the way for the two most productive years of her career, 1936 and 1937, in which she starred in no less than four timeless vehicles, each in its

NAUGHTY MARIETTA (1935). With Nelson Eddy

NAUGHTY MARIETTA (1935). *In the title role*

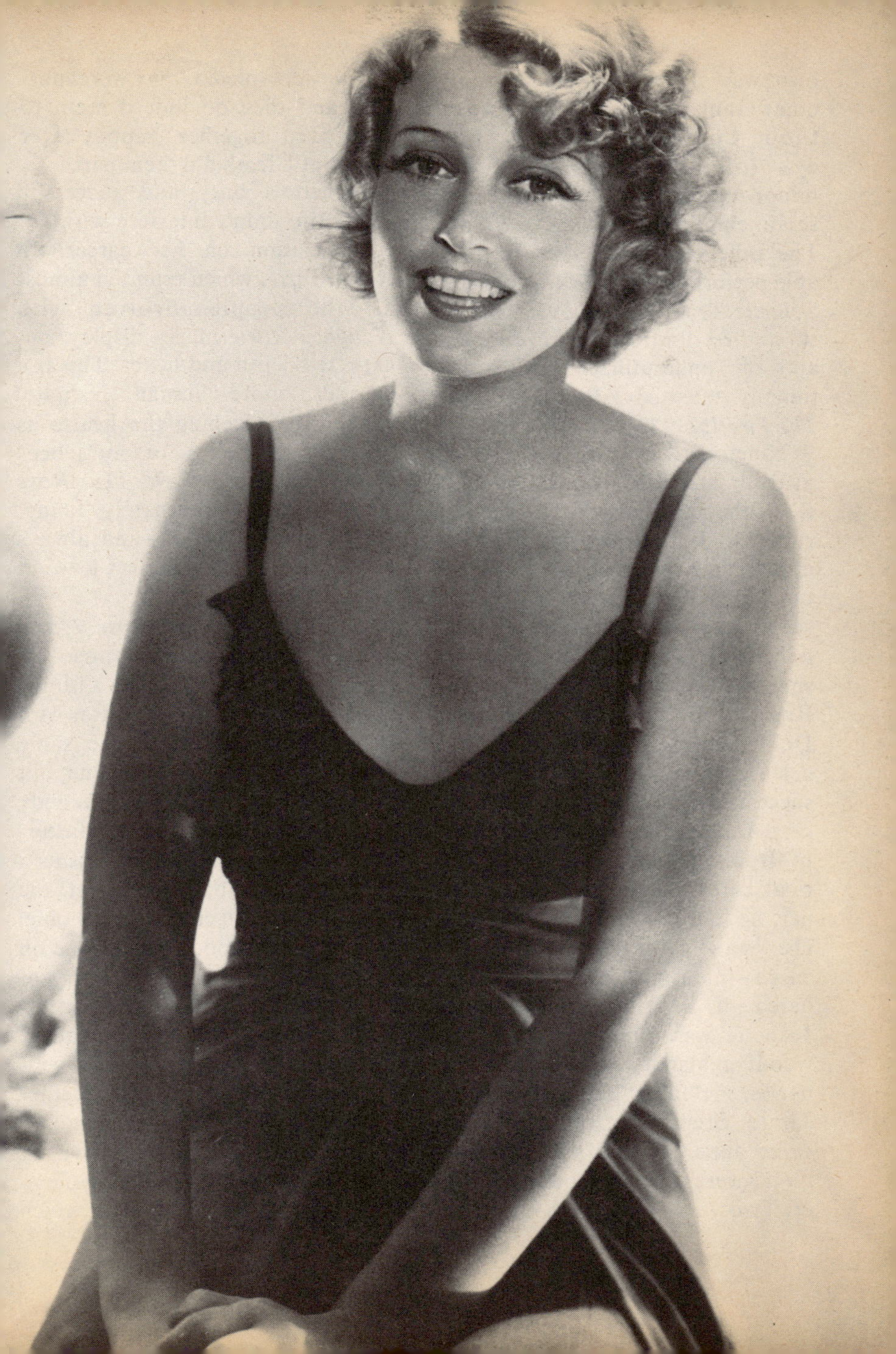

own way illustrating her extraordinary range and versatility. Two of them costarred Nelson Eddy—*Rose Marie* in 1936 and that minor masterpiece of schmaltz and sentimentality, *Maytime*, in 1937. The others featured such formidable performers as Clark Gable and Spencer Tracy, in the 1936 epic of sin and retribution, *San Francisco*, and the underutilized but exceptionally talented Allan Jones (in *The Firefly*, 1937).

Nineteen thirty-five was a good year for Jeanette, and she gloried in it. At the age of thirty-two, she was riding high in Hollywood, and her appearance reflected her good fortune. One of the reasons for her off-screen glow was her newest romantic interest, Gene Raymond, whom she had met at a party given by Rosie Dolly, one of the famous Dolly Sisters. Raymond was then costarring with Loretta Young in a successful Fox film, *Zoo in Budapest*. Like Jeanette, Gene, a native of Brooklyn, had aimed for a theatrical career at an early age. Like her, he had a doting stage mother. He was considered a good catch—pleasant and well-mannered, if a little stiff. Although Jeanette was often seen in Hollywood nightspots with other luminaries, including Nelson Eddy and James Stewart, it gradually became apparent that she and Raymond were serious about each other. Two years after *Naughty Marietta* was completed, they were married, and they do indeed seem to have lived together happily ever after, until death did them part.

Jeanette's busy and successful social life didn't interfere with her concentration on her career. In *Rose Marie*, which reunited almost all the people involved with *Naughty Marietta*, she displays unexpected depth and luster. This is a warmer, more human Jeanette, capable of reaching the hearts as well as the ears of audiences throughout the world. In *Rose Marie*, she is alternately funny, touching, and tender—and always believable. She is a perfect jewel in a perfect setting.

The ingredients of *Rose Marie* are very similar to those of *Naughty Marietta*. Each is a filmed version of a popular operetta, with the same director and the same stars. It was more of the same, but immeasurably improved. Woody Van Dyke's direction is faster-moving, better paced. Perhaps as a result of the expanded budget, the sets are no longer claustrophobic. Much of the shooting was done on location, with the lake country of California and Nevada substituting for the Canadian equivalent. Nelson is more relaxed and self-confident. Everything fits together like a well-planned jigsaw puzzle.

The story line has been vastly altered from that of the hyphenated stage hit *Rose-Marie*, which

ROSE MARIE (1936). With Reginald Owen (center)

ROSE MARIE (1936). With Nelson Eddy

had starred Dennis King on Broadway in 1924. In the original, the title character is a singer in a broken-down Canadian hotel who is reunited with her lover by a noble Mounted Policeman when he clears the hero of a murder charge. Although very important to the machinations of the plot, the Mountie is a supporting actor who serves as a catalyst for bringing the principals together.

In the much-improved 1936 screen version, the Mountie is the hero and is honor-bound to get his man, who happens to be the renegade criminal brother of the heroine, Marie de Flor, a famous Canadian opera singer. (The character of the heroine had been especially tailored by Francis Goodrich, Albert Hackett, and Alice Duer Miller to fit the talents of Grace Moore, who had been originally slated for the part. When the tremendous popularity of *Naughty Marietta* catapulted Jeanette into the leading role, it turned out that she had all the qualities of Miss Moore, plus a few of her very own.)

As the film opens, Jeanette displays both her clear operatic voice and her ever-improving acting. She is on stage, appearing opposite Allan Jones, by then an MGM contract player, in a scene from Gounod's *Romeo et Juliette*. She sings Juliet's familiar waltz song, which is followed by a montage of other scenes from the opera, and a snatch of the opera's finale. She and Jones take their curtain calls to thunderous applause. While the curtain is up, Jeanette curtsies gracefully and gratefully, the very picture of modest gratitude for the homage of the adoring audience. She smiles sweetly at her costar and bows demurely to the conductor. But behind the curtain and in surreptitious glares at the conductor she rails at everyone in sight, and she makes it clear that she is displeased with everything but her own performance. It is a clever and hilarious reprise of the opening sequence of *Oh, For a Man*.

In her dressing room, a rich and rather ridiculous suitor (David Niven, then known as David Nivens) is waiting, having followed her from New York. After getting rid of him quickly, the prima donna confides to her maid (Una Merkel) that the only man she has ever really cared for is her brother, Jack, who is a convicted criminal now serving time in prison.

When her nervous manager (Reginald Owen) comes in to tell her that the premier of Quebec (Alan Mowbray) would consider it a privilege to meet the great Marie de Flor, she arranges to hold a private dinner for him so that she can try to wangle a pardon for her wayward brother.

At the party, where Jeanette sings a pleasant ballad, "Pardon

Me, Madame," an unexpected guest arrives with an urgent message. It is Boniface (George Regas), an Indian, who has come to tell her that her brother Jack has escaped from prison and killed a Mountie. Jack has been wounded and badly needs her help. Horrified, Jeanette leaves her guests, gets hold of all the money she can find, and prepares to follow Boniface into the Canadian wilds to find her brother and offer him comfort and cash.

Somewhere in the lake country of Canada, a handsome sergeant leads a troop of Royal Canadian Mounted Police in a spirited rendition of "The Mounties." We soon learn that this man, Sergeant Bruce (Eddy), has been assigned to apprehend the killer, John Flower.

That night, Marie and Boniface reach town. Boniface runs off with the naive girl's money, leaving her penniless. Desperate, Marie wanders into the only café, where she asks for a job. She notices a singer being pelted with cash by the motley group of customers, and is told that she can try the same thing if she wants to, and pocket all the money that's thrown to her. Feebly and futilely, she tries to out-sing

ROSE MARIE (1936). With George Regas and Nelson Eddy

ROSE MARIE (1936). With James Stewart

and out-shimmy Gilda Gray, the bona fide queen of the shimmy, who is infectiously vulgar in her small role as the café singer Belle. Marie attempts "Dinah" and "Some of These Days," then flees from the café, close to tears.

But Sergeant Bruce has heard her and follows her out into the dirt road. He tries to comfort her, then gets her to go to his office and report the robbery. She tells him her name is Rose Marie. Between puffs on his pipe, he says, "I always thought your name was just *Marie de Flor.*" He is, of course, an opera lover, and recognized her as soon as he heard her sing.

The remainder of the movie concerns the Mountie's attempts to find the runaway killer, his romancing of the steadily thawing prima donna, and his dawning realization that the man he is pursuing is the brother of the woman he loves. Along the way, there is one intriguing moment after another.

Paddling Rose Marie in a canoe across a shimmering lake in the moonlight, Sgt. Bruce launches into the familiar "Rose Marie." She is impressed with his voice but a little incredulous at his ability to compose a song on the spot. He explains that this is his standard courting song. It worked with Annabelle and Caroline—"Caroline, I love you,"—but it didn't work with Maude. "But then," he says after a pause, "nothing worked with Maude."

At an Indian festival, seeking the treacherous Boniface, they take time out to watch a rather pallid dance choreographed by Chester Hale to "Totem Tom Tom." Later, they join voices in the unashamedly corny "Indian Love Call," although they never sing nose-to-nose as in the dozens of parodies to come.

Rose Marie has fallen in love with the handsome sergeant—and his voice. She asks him to give up the Mounties and return with her to become an opera singer, but he refuses. He belongs here, he says, and argues reasonably that when she gets back to the city, she'll remember him only for what he is—"a policeman."

Sergeant Bruce later follows Rose Marie, led by a reluctant Boniface, to a shack where her brother is hiding out. She has only a brief reunion with Jack before the Mountie interrupts. In spite of his love for Rose Marie, he must do his duty and take Jack into custody. But the young man, brilliantly played by James Stewart in his second film role, is strangely unrepentant. He can't help himself, he explains. He has always loved excitement. Sergeant Bruce takes him off to prison. It is a disturbing scene, with a ring of truth uncommon in operettas.

Unlike *Naughty Marietta*, *Rose Marie* needs no allowance from today's audiences. The film is marred only by a weak and unmotivated ending. Marie, unnerved by her brother's arrest and the loss of her loved one, goes into seclusion in a hunting lodge. Her manager calls for Sergeant Bruce. He arrives, they join in a reprise of "Indian Love Call," and everything seems happily resolved. Not a word about her brother or her career. She is now apparently content to spend the rest of her life with her stalwart sweetheart in the Canadian wilderness.

Rose Marie was even more popular than *Naughty Marietta*. It was one of the top-grossing films of the year. Jeanette and Nelson were called the "perfect team" by the *New York Daily News*, and *The New York Times* thought they were "fully as delightful a combination" as they had been in *Naughty Marietta*. *Variety* called the film a "box-office honey."

Today's moviegoers who are lucky enough to see a reissue of this grand movie will readily see why it was and remains so popular. Either under its original name or its "television title," *Indian Love Call* (which began appearing after MGM's 1954 CinemaScope ver-

At the piano in her home

On the set of SAN FRANCISCO (1936) with director W. S. Van Dyke

sion, starring Ann Blyth and Howard Keel, was released), it's a delightful experience.

The formula had worked twice, so it was inevitable that MGM would want still another reprise of the now fabulously popular singing duo. The studio bosses approached Jeanette with a remake of Sigmund Romberg's perennial favorite, *Maytime*, but the actress had ideas of her own. She had been approached by a writer named Robert Hopkins with an idea for a story based loosely on the life of a man named Wilson Mizner. Hopkins had changed the name of the leading character to Blackie Norton, and had created a particularly appealing female character named Mary Blake for a pivotal role. Irving Thalberg was enthusiastic, and asked Hopkins and his friend Anita Loos to write the screenplay. They called it *San Francisco*.

Thalberg became very ill before production could begin, but it was he who persuaded MGM to go ahead with the project and helped Jeanette convince the box-office king, Clark Gable, to play Blackie Norton.

Gable, having just completed the great epic *Mutiny on the Bounty*, wanted a rest and told Jeanette he'd rather go hunting, but she begged him simply to read the script. He did, and still wasn't convinced. All he had to do, he thought, was stand there while Jeanette sang and everybody applauded. The script was rewritten, Spencer Tracy was brought in to play a two-fisted priest, and Gable reluctantly accepted the role of Blackie.

Jeanette wanted a change of pace. Louis B. Mayer wanted, as usual, a box-office blockbuster. Both of these strong-willed people got what they wanted. *San Francisco* had everything—a simple-minded story of sin and retribution, demonstrating the often-repeated Mayer moral that there can be no happiness without God, a truly memorable earthquake sequence, and three of the most popular stars of the time—MacDonald, Gable, and Tracy.

As directed by the dependable W. S. Van Dyke, the opening scene sets the somewhat sanctimonious tone. A title on parchment tells us that San Francisco today is "a queen among seaports ... industrious, mature, respectable..." but was once "vulgar and magnificent" prior to "exactly 5:13 A.M. April 18, 1906." At this point, the parchment bursts into flames.

It is New Year's Eve, December 31, 1905. We are introduced to Blackie Norton, in full regalia, including white tie and black cape. Immediately, we see the kind of city this is. A horse-drawn fire truck whizzes through the streets. Hitching a ride on the truck, Blackie saunters into his nightspot, the Paradise, where his female

SAN FRANCISCO (1936). With Clark Gable

SAN FRANCISCO (1936). With Jessie Ralph

employees and customers alike shower him with unseemly affection. While a "society" lady at one of the tables kisses Blackie passionately, her husband is intent on grabbing a scantily clad dancer. This is the Barbary Coast, that Hollywood symbol of sin and decadence.

An innocent young girl who wants to be a singer shows up at Blackie's place. It is Jeanette, as Mary Blake, whose room has been destroyed in the fire to which the truck had been racing. She auditions falteringly, but Blackie, after asking to see her legs, offers her a job at the fabulous sum of seventy-five dollars a week. She faints. Matt, the resident song-and-dance man, says if *he* were offered seventy-five a week, he'd drop *dead*.

It turns out that Mary is a new kind of girl for Blackie. She is the daughter of a parson, and comes from a small town in Colorado. When Blackie attempts a pass, he is rebuffed. She locks the door to her bedroom. As Blackie prepares to turn in for the night, he looks at himself in the mirror and says, "Good night, sucker."

The next morning, we meet Spencer Tracy as Father Tim Mullin. Blackie and Father Tim spar in a gym, Gable looking rather puffy in his bare chest and tights. A group of businessmen come in and ask Blackie to run for supervisor so the city can get decent fire laws and unseat some of the corrupt politicians now in power. Father Tim persuades Blackie to accept, relying on his innate decency and his love for a fight.

Learning of Blackie's decision to run for office, a tough but elegant socialite businessman from "uptown," Jack Burley (played stiffly by veteran actor Jack Holt) arrives at Blackie's to persuade him to change his mind. An honest supervisor would mean that he, as well as other less-than-law-abiding businessmen, would lose a great deal of money. Burley brings with him, for some unexplained reason, an impresario from the Tivoli Opera.

At Blackie's, the impresario is accosted by the piano-playing "professor" (Al Shean, an excellent character actor once known as half of the vaudeville team of Gallagher and Shean). The professor begs them to listen to the café's new singer.

When Jeanette comes on and sings, the impresario is impressed and asks to meet her. She comes over and tells him that they might have met under better circumstances. She had turned up six days in a row at the Tivoli Opera, vainly hoping for an audition.

Burley and the impresario offer Mary a contract to sing at the opera, but Blackie triumphantly explains that she has already signed a two-year contract with *him*. (The crowd at the Paradise particularly loves her spirited singing of "San Francisco.") He then orders Mary to get out and sing at a place around the corner, which turns out to be the mission run by Father Tim.

Father Tim and Mary immediately take to each other. Tim tells her how he and Blackie grew up together, and are still great friends although their philosophies are entirely different. Sounding the theme of the movie, he tells Mary she's in the wickedest, most corrupt city in America. "Sometimes I wonder what the end is going to be," he intones. Since everybody in the audience knows the answer, having seen the introduction to the film, the only real question is how long it will take before we get a chance to see the earthquake.

Nowadays, it seems to take a very long time. In between, we have to suffer through Mary's lovers' tiffs with Blackie, a few operatic sequences, and a scene in Mary's dressing room at the opera house where Father Tim confronts Blackie with his wickedness. By this time, Blackie has confessed to Mary that he loves her and agrees to marry her, but he wants to take her away from the opera house and back to the Paradise. To Father Tim, this seems like a fate worse than death. "You can't marry a

SAN FRANCISCO (1936). With Clark Gable and Spencer Tracy

SAN FRANCISCO (1936). With Clark Gable

woman and sell her immortal soul," he says. Blackie understandably takes offense, and punches Father Tim in the nose. When Tim refuses to fight back, we know that retribution must be near.

Later, Burley arranges to take his favorite opera singer to the Chicken's Ball, a Barbary Coast competition in which the first prize is ten thousand dollars "for artistic achievement." The prize has been won by the Paradise for the past three years, and Blackie has given the money to "the little mugs down here on the Coast." The conniving Burley assures Mary that Blackie won't be there, not telling her that he has arranged for the Paradise to be shuttered for selling liquor without a license, and has also bought off Blackie's former supporters.

At the Chicken's Ball, the audience is rowdy and noisy. A man drags a willing entertainer from a dressing room while his wife looks on, amused. An old flame of Blackie's appears at Burley's table and tells him what she thinks of him. For the first time, Mary learns about Burley's nefarious machinations.

The master of ceremonies announces there will be no entry from the Paradise this year. Mary springs to her feet. "I represent the Paradise!", she exclaims as she walks to the stage.

Blackie, who has come in quietly and is about to leave, turns to watch. When Mary announces she will sing "San Francisco," the

SAN FRANCISCO (1936). The earthquake sequence

Nelson Eddy

MAYTIME (1937). With Nelson Eddy

crowd goes wild. She sings the familiar words, at first slowly and stirringly, then in what she evidently considered a torchy, throbbing version. Jeanette MacDonald was never competition for Al Jolson, and she shouldn't have attempted this totally inappropriately style. Van Dyke warned her against it, but she persisted. He was proved right, and she admitted later that it had been a mistake. But movie audiences of the time thought it was terrific.

Mary wins the competition. But Blackie strides up to the stage, takes the trophy cup from her, and throws it away. "I don't need this kind of dough," he says.

The revenge for this ungracious conduct comes immediately from on high. As Mary struggles to the door, fighting back tears, a low rumble is heard. The noise increases, mounting to a roar. The chandelier sways. Glasses on the tables quiver. The people freeze with horror. The floor begins to shiver. Then a wall trembles. Mary screams and staggers toward Blackie, but Burley grabs her protectively and guides her to the stairs. They disappear in the dust which covers the entire room.

A balcony collapses, sending patrons sprawling. Screams mingle

MAYTIME (1937). With Nelson Eddy in an operatic sequence

MAYTIME (1937). As Marcia Mornay, in costume for a performance of the opera "Les Huguenots"

MAYTIME (1937). With Rafaela Ottiano

with the roars of the earth. Then, abruptly, there is silence.

Blackie, almost buried under bricks, struggles to his feet. He pushes aside beams and other debris, helping injured people as he clambers out of the building. Outside, people in their nightclothes are screaming for help, or crying out the names of friends or relatives. Blackie turns at the sound of his name, and he and a passerby try to drag two men from under a pile of debris. Then, just as suddenly as the silence, another roar begins to build. Houses sway. Whole housefronts drop away. We hear screams, the yapping of dogs, as an entire city goes mad with hysteria.

As Blackie continues his stumbling search for Mary, a girl says she knows where Jack Burley is. She points to a pile of bricks, the remains of a wall, from which Burley's head and arm stick out. Blackie feverishly digs into the pile.

It's obvious Mary's body isn't there. As Blackie runs blindly on, he steps over a small crack in the street. The crack widens until it becomes a gaping fissure, with pipes spouting water. A man falls into the widening hole, while another man grabs the edge frantically, trying not to fall. Downed wires sputter dangerously and wooden debris explodes into flames. A roaring fire begins to race down the streets, destroying everything in its path, including entire houses. Firemen arrive on screeching trucks, but when they attach their hoses to the hydrants, only a few trickles of water emerge. There is no way to fight the rampaging blaze.

After this harrowing, unforgettable sequence, the film moves rapidly to its stirring conclusion. With Father Tim's help, the repentant Blackie finds Mary at the top of a hill. Silhouetted against the sky, with a group of ragged children surrounding her, she is trying to comfort the mother of a dead child with a moving rendition of "Nearer, My God, To Thee." The burning city is spread out below. It is enough to make the most persistent sinner turn to God, which Blackie promptly does, on his knees, tears flowing. (They say that Gable was unable to conjure up enough emotion to cry on cue, so he conveniently turns his back. When the camera focuses in on him, tears—or their Hollywood equivalent—are indeed streaming down his cheeks.)

Meanwhile, the army has been busy dynamiting entire blocks to prevent the flames from spreading. The tactic has succeeded. Somebody shouts, "The fire's out." Cries of "Halleleujah" are heard. Somebody shouts, "We'll build a new San Francisco."

To the strains of "The Battle Hymn of the Republic," the people of San Francisco march, arm in arm, toward the future. Prominent

MAYTIME (1937). With John Barrymore

among them are Blackie and Mary. Just behind them, as befits his billing, is Father Tim. As the marchers look out over the stricken city, a new metropolis rises from the ashes. It is the modern, sleek San Francisco of 1936, with automobiles, buses, the Golden Gate Bridge, and all the other signs of modernity so dear to the hearts of Americans in the thirties.

If *San Francisco* today seems slow going for at least the first third of the movie, the moviegoers of 1936 found it fascinating. The real star is the earthquake, a brilliant and innovative sequence never to be equalled, even by the special-effects staffs of the vaunted "disaster" movies of the seventies.

Jeanette and Gable didn't really suit each other very well, and Gable's part was full of awkward slang, awkwardly delivered. Even the King had trouble with lines like, "I'm crazy about ya, kid, ya know that?" Spencer Tracy walked through his role, seldom changing his pace or expression. Even Jeanette was comparatively lifeless in this turgid morality tale. Yet, with all its obvious faults, *San Francisco* is still worth seeing. Like William Boehnel of the *New York World Telegram* in 1936, viewers in the seventies can easily succumb to its "good old-fashioned hokum."

Other critics, and the public at large, were much more lavish in their praise. Frank S. Nugent of *The New York Times* thought it "a near-perfect illustration of the cinema's inherent and acquired ability to absorb and digest other art forms and convert them into its own sinews."

Louis B. Mayer was overjoyed. The film netted more than two million dollars, when a million dollars was *really* a lot of money. It was nominated for six Academy Awards, named one of the top ten films of 1936 by many critics, and received the *Photoplay* magazine Gold Medal as Best Picture of the Year.

Jeanette had proved her point. She had shown she could be a big draw without benefit of either the tried-and-true operetta format or the support of Nelson Eddy.

But she didn't intend to abandon her former environment. With her wages at an all-time high and her popularity at its peak, she happily went back to the studio to begin filming *Maytime*. She and Eddy were to star, with Edmund Goulding as director, and with Paul Lukas and Frank Morgan in important supporting roles. After shooting began, however, Thalberg, who had been in charge of production although he was too ill to work, died. In September, 1936, production was halted. When

MAYTIME (1937). With Nelson Eddy

shooting resumed, there was a new director and a whole new cast of supporting actors. Louis B. Mayer wanted his *own* version with his *own* carefully selected cast, and that's what he got. As he proved in many other instances, Mayer was a shrewd judge of material and talent.

If *Merry Widow* is a soufflé and *Rose Marie* a hearty beef stew of a movie, *Maytime* is a sugary confection that by all rights should be indigestible but turns out to be irresistibly delicious.

The screen version uses very little of the music composed for the 1917 operetta by Sigmund Romberg. Instead, it relies on a mélange of traditional melodies, operatic arias, and a few Romberg tunes to provide the underpinning for a superbly overdone tale of tragic and tempestuous love. In the opening scene, Jeanette again displays her expanding versatility as an actress. She plays an old woman, known only as Miss Morrison, who lives in virtual seclusion with an attentive elderly maid. Supporting herself with a cane, Miss Morrison strolls slowly through a throng of turn-of-the-century May Day celebrants—children dancing around a Maypole, young lovers walking hand in hand. She is calm and reflective, but an air of sadness surrounds her. Never stooping to exaggeration or caricature, Jeanette, in a few brief minutes, faultlessly establishes the character of this dignified lady. (Her acting and makeup were so convincing that many moviegoers, and even some of her friends, refused to believe that this frail old woman was really the vivacious Jeanette MacDonald.)

Miss Morrison shares a bench with a distraught young man (Tom Brown) who pours out his heart to her. It seems his fiancée, Barbara (Lynne Carver) has been offered an opportunity to go off to New York and become a great opera star—or so she has been assured by a visiting impresario.

After overhearing Barbara and her young man quarreling later that day, Miss Morrison invites the aspiring singer into her garden, full of trees, dappled sunlight, and gently falling blossoms. She wants to tell Barbara a story. She begins, "It was many, many years ago. I was very young. It was in the court of Louis Napoleon."

We are immediately transported to that opulent court, courtesy of appropriate ballroom music and splendidly designed sets by Cedric Gibbons. At the court ball, we are introduced to the lovely young singer Marcia Mornay (Jeanette, looking younger and fresher than ever), escorted by her brooding coach and personal manager, Nickolai Nazaroff (John Barrymore). Later, she meets the penniless American baritone, Paul Allison (Eddy), who eventually wins her heart. They spend one glorious May Day together. Paul sings her a beautiful song, "Sweetheart, sweetheart, sweetheart ... Will you remember the day/When we were happy in May?" She promises to remember always, but, after a mellifluous montage showing how she becomes a famous opera star, she agrees to marry the possessive Nazaroff—partly out of gratitude, partly to further her career.

The marriage is doomed from the beginning, with Nazaroff's fierce possessiveness causing continual friction. Years later, learning she is planning to run away with her only true love, Paul, Nazaroff visits his rival. "I'm giving Marcia her freedom, and you yours," he says. As the sound of an exploding bullet is heard, Marcia comes rushing up the steps. Paul dies with his head cradled in Marcia's lap. With his last breath, he tells Marcia that the one day they spent together has lasted him all his life. Snow drifts against the windowpane. The snow turns into swirling white blossoms, and we are once again in Miss Morrison's sunny garden.

Young Barbara gets the message. She will remain with the man she loves. As Miss Morrison leans back against an apple tree, satisfied, life leaves her. In death, she and Paul are reunited. The form of the beautiful Marcia Mornay emerges from Miss Morrison's frail, lifeless body.

With ventriloquist Edgar Bergen, dummy Charlie McCarthy, husband Gene Raymond, and Nelson Eddy

THE FIREFLY (1937). As Nina Maria

Jeanette and Nelson literally walk through the air to heavenly bliss as broken blossoms fall into a meandering stream and spell out The End. Described baldly, the scene sounds unbearably mawkish. In context, it is touching and tender, a perfect ending for a nearly perfect film.

Maytime is a triumph for Jeanette, but she shares honors with Nelson, who is charming and casual as the carefree American, and with the formidable John Barrymore. By this time, Barrymore was visibly on his way to self-destruction, wasted by drink and indulgence. In some scenes, he could barely stand up, and Jeanette was careful to avoid his fetid breath and wandering hands. He read his lines from gigantic cue cards. But somehow, even these defects lent credibility to his portrayal of the doomed impresario who loses the one thing he loves. His vibrant voice and piercing eyes, cleverly accented by director Leonard, dominate his every scene.

Like Jeanette's two previous films, *Maytime* was a well-deserved critical and box-office success. In January, 1937, she and Nelson were named "best singers in the movies" by *Modern Screen* magazine. She was an unquestioned superstar, long before that term was invented.

By the time *Maytime* was released, Jeanette's sister Blossom and her husband, Warren Rock, were also living in Hollywood after having appeared together as a traveling vaudeville team. Blossom became an MGM contract player, changed her stage name to Marie Blake, and appeared in a supporting role in *Mannequin*, starring Joan Crawford and Spencer Tracy. She later had a continuing role as Sally, the switchboard operator in the popular Dr. Kildare series starring Lew Ayres. The oldest MacDonald sister, Elsie, was back in Philadelphia, where she owned and operated the kind of dancing and acting school she and her sisters had attended so many years earlier. She seldom visited her younger sister in Hollywood.

The Rocks were among the star-studded guests who attended Jeanette's elaborate Hollywood-style wedding to Gene Raymond in June, 1937. Among the other guests were Louis B. Mayer, Nelson Eddy, Allan Jones, Mr. and Mrs. Basil Rathbone, and Harold Lloyd. Jeanette's mother was ecstatic, but Gene's mother stayed home. She considered Jeanette a cradle-snatcher; her beloved Gene, at 28, was five years younger than his bride.

The new Mrs. Raymond had already started filming *The Firefly*, with Allan Jones in the leading male role. Nelson was available, but even his staunchest supporters couldn't envisage him as the dash-

THE FIREFLY (1937). With Warren William

ing Don Diego, who had to ride, sing, trade quips, and fight with equal ease. Robert Z. Leonard was again chosen as director. Both he and Jeanette liked and respected the young tenor, and Jeanette openly looked forward to the new partnership. In spite of her recent success in *San Francisco*, she was still a little fearful of being identified only as half of the MacDonald-Eddy pairing. Although Jones was still comparatively unknown, she insisted that he receive equal treatment. She was the star, and everyone knew it, but, as Jones liked to recall gratefully, she insisted that Leonard divide the closeups between them.

As totally revised for the film version, Rudolf Friml's *The Firefly* is an action-packed if somewhat complicated tale about a Spanish dancer, Nina Maria, who is recruited to spy for her country during the Napoleonic Wars. Don Diego, the hero, a disguised French officer, is both her suitor and her adversary. With its unexpected twists and subterfuges, *The Firefly* might easily have been made into a serious spy melodrama. As it is, it's a humdinger of a musical, spiced with well-staged battle scenes, wit, and beautiful melodies. Jones, an excellent horseman and ingratiat-

THE FIREFLY (1937). With Allan Jones

THE GIRL OF THE GOLDEN WEST (1938). As Mary Robbins

ing actor, more than lives up to the faith shown in him by Jeanette and Leonard.

The hit song of the movie, concocted especially for the occasion by studio composers Chet Forrest and Bob Wright from a previously neglected piano piece by Friml, is the catchy, hummable "Donkey Serenade." Don Diego sings it to an unresponsive Jeanette, then to her mule, while he is on horseback and she is riding in a stagecoach. Portions of the sequence are unbearably arch, particularly when a requisitely cute little boy and other passengers, including Jeanette, bob their heads in unison in time to the rhythm, but Jones is delightful. His fall off his horse at the end of the number lends just the right touch of self-mocking good humor. As for Jeanette, she had never looked more beautiful, or acted and sung with more vivacity. Between them, she and Jones lent utter enchantment to this beguiling film.

But in Hollywood, success is measured in relative terms. *The Firefly* didn't gross as well as the three previous MacDonald-Eddy vehicles. To Louis B. Mayer, who had never liked the independent, intelligent Jones, the meaning was clear. The public wanted Jeanette and Nelson together. So Allan Jones, the possessor of a style and casual forcefulness Nelson Eddy could never match, sat out the remainder of his MGM contract. And Jeanette, bowing to studio pressure, went on to make five more pictures with Nelson, none of which faintly approached the zest and sparkle of the infectious *Rose Marie* or the romantic charm of *Maytime*.

For Jeanette and Nelson, their joint appearance in *The Girl of the Golden West*, directed by Leonard, was the beginning of the end. Jeanette had again voiced her preference for Allan Jones to play opposite her in this hokey version of an old David Belasco melodrama, reasoning that the hero, Ramerez, an outlaw with a heart of gold, was similar in style to the swashbuckling Don Diego of *The Firefly*. But Mayer was adamant, and Eddy was overjoyed to be playing opposite Jeanette again. His interim feature without her, *Rosalie*, featuring songs by Cole Porter and the able assistance of Eleanor Powell and Ilona Massey, had been a lukewarm success, but he was anxious to rekindle the sparks he thought were guaranteed when he and the beguiling redhead appeared together on the screen.

Nelson was, as Jeanette had thought, unsuited for the role. He looked pudgy and acted sluggishly. Jeanette, as a rough-and-ready frontier woman, wasn't much better, and Walter Pidgeon as the ambiguous antagonist, Jack Rance, seemed understandably uncomfortable. Not all the reviews were

THE GIRL OF THE GOLDEN WEST (1938). With Walter Pidgeon

THE GIRL OF THE GOLDEN WEST (1938). With Nelson Eddy

SWEETHEARTS (1938). With Nelson Eddy

marsh, but *Time* magazine commented unkindly on Nelson's "roly-poly pinkness" and the *New York World Telegram* called Jeanette's acting "a little bit embarrassing."

Later in 1938, they partially redeemed themselves by relaxing a bit in their roles as a bickering musical comedy team in *Sweethearts*, directed by reliable W. S. Van Dyke. Their first in Technicolor, the film has the advantage of a literate screenplay by Dorothy Parker and Alan Campbell and some lively tunes by Victor Herbert. Ray Bolger contributes his impish presence and dancing feet, and joins Jeanette in a pleasant little Dutch dance number called, appropriately enough, "Wooden Shoes." Both costars look right at home in color and contemporary clothes, which help to mask the bulges around Eddy's middle that had been so obvious in his most recent costume films. *Sweethearts* is not a great movie, but it still provides, as Bosley Crowther wrote in *The New York Times*, an evening of "sweet, theatrical sentiment."

After *Sweethearts*, the film careers of both Jeanette and Nelson went downhill fast. Both were still under contract to MGM, but Mayer, in a sudden and illogical change of philosophy, decided that he could profitably separate the two stars, arguing that each could easily "carry" a film with lesser-known supporting actors. Nelson went on to make two less-than-mediocre features, *Balalaika* (1939), costarring the beautiful Ilona Massey, and a synthetic historical pageant, *Let Freedom Ring* (1939).

Jeanette's next film, sans Eddy, was *Broadway Serenade*, in which she played an opera singer who marries a down-and-out composer (Lew Ayres), forced to take a temporary job as a pianist in a barroom. Predictably, the two quarrel and are divorced, but they get together again when she stars in her former husband's Broadway extravaganza. The lethargy of the two stars was matched by the slow pace of director Robert Z. Leonard. *The New York Times*, in this case speaking for the majority, called *Broadway Serenade* "the biggest bad show of the year."

Fortunately for Jeanette, her declining movie career didn't interfere with her personal appeal. She whiled away the time between films by appearing on many radio broadcasts, and her records continued to sell well. Her frequent song recitals were always sold out.

By 1940, the unpredictable Louis B. Mayer decided he wanted to pair his favorite team once again. He reached into the MGM shelf and pulled out *New Moon*, another familiar Sigmund Romberg operetta, and tried desperately to turn out a virtual carbon copy of the earliest

MacDonald-Eddy hit, *Naughty Marietta*. As in *Naughty Marietta*, Jeanette played a runaway French noblewoman wooed and won by a rugged adventurer. As in *Naughty Marietta*, Nelson got to sing a stirring march song, in this case "Stout-Hearted Men." The only essential differences were the director, Robert Z. Leonard, and the ages of the principal characters. That was enough. The formula didn't work the second time around. Jeanette and Nelson were apparently encouraged by Leonard to appear young and bright, and as a result they both mug and overact in almost every scene. *Times* critic Bosley Crowther commented a little ambiguously on their "winsome but slightly ponderous charm" and was directly on target when he wrote of his suspicion that "this sort of sugar-coated musical fiction has seen its better days."

Worse was yet to come. It's said that Noël Coward cried when he saw MGM's synthetic 1940 version of his anglicized operetta in the Viennese style, *Bitter Sweet*. They weren't tears of joy. Admirers of Jeanette MacDonald who see revivals of this fatuous film today may well shed a few tears of their own when they reflect on what happened to the radiant actress in the few short years since *Rose Marie* and *The Firefly*.

Woody Van Dyke tried hard to push the scenes along, but could do very little to overcome the vapid script by Lesser Samuels and the awkward acting of his two principals. Both Jeanette and Nelson

SWEETHEARTS (1938). With Nelson Eddy in a musical number

BROADWAY SERENADE (1939). With Lew Ayres

seem overaged, overweight, and overly made-up. The harsh lighting and excessive cosmetics which marred many of the Technicolor movies of the early forties exaggerate Jeanette's age, make her richness seem pathetic, and call undue attention to her unceasing facial reactions. In supporting roles, even such reliable performers as George Sanders and Ian Hunter seem stiff. Only Herman Bing, in a brief but hilarious scene in which he is almost persuaded to trade a scrawny chicken for singing lessons for his untalented daughter, brings a welcome breath of life to this tired tale.

Bitter Sweet lost money and that was *really* something new. Critics called the film "embarrassing." Jeanette was thirty-seven, an age in which many actresses just begin to hit their stride. But her best days were obviously behind her. Even so, she kept on trying. In 1941, she and her husband, Gene Raymond, co-starred in their only film together, *Smilin' Through*, directed by Frank Borzage. It was another disaster. Utilizing the same script written only nine years before in a version starring Jeanette's friend, Norma Shearer, the 1941 film simply added some ballads and traditional songs to take advantage of

BROADWAY SERENADE (1939). As Mary Hale

NEW MOON (1940). With Nelson Eddy

Jeanette's voice. The story and most of the dialogue were absolutely identical. *Smilin' Through* is a sentimental melodrama about a young Irish girl separated from her loved one by war and the interference of her old guardian (Brian Aherne). The guardian has bitter memories of his beloved bride being slain at the altar by the lover's father, many years before. Jeanette is both the girl and the murdered bride (whose ectoplasmic spirit appears periodically) and Raymond is both the lover and his father.

Seen today, *Smilin' Through* is pleasant enough, if a little ponderous. In 1941, it was roundly roasted by the critics and stoutly resisted by film audiences. It was called "dull," a "tearjerker," a "museum piece." Perhaps we're more tolerant of museum pieces these days. But even the most tolerant of modern-day moviegoers will find the love scenes unconvincing, and Gene Raymond makes Eddy, who was frequently criticized for his unbending stiffness, seem almost dynamic by comparison. Aherne received some favorable notices but, in general, *Smilin' Through* was yet another embarrassment.

Nelson wasn't faring much better. His most recent film, *The Chocolate Soldier*, costarring the pretty young opera singer Risë Stevens, had also been a dud at the box office. Eddy was understandably peeved, since he had displayed unexpected comic gifts as an actor-husband who makes love to his own wife while masquerading as an improbable Cossack officer. The critics had liked Miss Stevens in her movie debut, and many had mentioned Eddy's clever impersonation, but audiences stayed away in droves.

By 1942, Jeanette MacDonald and Nelson Eddy were having their artistic problems, separately and together. It was apparent that the MacDonald-Eddy phenomenon had run its course, from instant popularity to worldwide adulation to faintly amused tolerance. In six short years, both appeared to have worn out their youth and freshness. Audiences would no longer flock to see their vehicles on the strength of the combined names. But Jeanette, Nelson, and MGM decided to try again, just one more time.

The comeback vehicle was to be *I Married an Angel*, which had been kicking around the MGM studios since the early thirties. Back then, the Rodgers and Hart musical, with a screenplay by Anita Loos, had been rejected as being too suggestive. The faintly risqué plot concerns a beautiful young angel who loses her virginity, and her wings, when she marries a very human playboy. The stage version, produced in 1938, had been only a

NEW MOON (1940). With H. B. Warner

NEW MOON (1940). As Marianne de Beaumanoir

BITTER SWEET (1940). Performing in a musical number

BITTER SWEET (1940). With Lynne Carver and Nelson Eddy

SMILIN' THROUGH (1941). With Brian Aherne

SMILIN' THROUGH (1941). With Gene Raymond

I MARRIED AN ANGEL (1942). With Nelson Eddy

mild success, but the story now seemed perfect for Jeanette and Nelson. She would be radiant and vivacious, and he would be allowed to show his age as an admittedly middle-aged playboy. Woody Van Dyke, then a major in the army, was brought in to direct, Bob Wright and Chet Forrest supplied additional songs, and producer Hunt Stromberg went out of his way to provide expensive and somewhat surrealistic sets.

It would be pleasant to report that the last collaboration of Jeanette MacDonald and Nelson Eddy was a huge success, and that they bowed out together in honor, warmed by cheers and adulation. Unfortunately, that wasn't the case. Nelson Eddy said it best: "Everybody on the lot told us it was either going to be the best picture we ever did, or the worst. It was the worst. It took the studio years to figure out how to present it without offending anybody and then they slashed it to pieces. When we finally finished it, it was a horrible mess."

It's hard to explain the sudden and almost unparalleled popularity of these two attractive performers, or their equally sudden fall from grace with both critics and the public. Jeanette MacDonald and Nelson Eddy were alike in many ways, but different in many others. Both received their early training and experience in Philadelphia. Both remained married to the same mate for twenty-seven years. Neither had any children. Both were dedicated and professional.

Jeanette, however, always thought of herself as a performer, an entertainer who could dance a little, act well, and sing better than most. Nelson considered himself a singer who had the mixed fortune to become a matinee idol and movie star. He never completely adjusted himself to becoming the object of female adulation or the target of well-aimed barbs from sarcastic observers.

Their screen personalities, largely because of the influence of Louis B. Mayer, lacked the contrasting qualities that distinguished the MacDonald-Chevalier collaborations. When they sang, they frequently sang *together*, their voices blending almost too sweetly. When they were good, they were very very good, as in *Rose Marie* and *Maytime*. When they were bad, as when they pretended to be a pair of happy kids when in reality they were approaching middle age, they were embarrassing.

Jeanette could easily have had a successful career on her own.

I MARRIED AN ANGEL (1942). With Inez Cooper, Nelson Eddy and Binnie Barnes

Nelson never made a really good picture without Jeanette. To this day, Allan Jones bemoans the accident of fate which prevented him from being co-starred with Jeanette in *Naughty Marietta*. He believes, and he may be right, that an early MacDonald-Jones pairing might have lasted longer and been even more successful than the Jeanette-Nelson combination.

Jeanette MacDonald's next film for MGM, also released in 1942, was *Cairo*, a low-budget spy film which couldn't decide whether it was a drama with comic overtones or an out-and-out spoof. Co-starring Robert Young and directed by Jeanette's old friend Woody Van Dyke, *Cairo* was modest in both its intentions and its reception. Its one note of distinction was an Ethel Waters duet with Dooley Wilson.

I Married an Angel was Nelson Eddy's last picture for MGM. The following year, he played the romantic lead in a satisfactory Technicolor version of the old thriller, *The Phantom of the Opera*, a Universal film with an effectively muted performance by Claude Rains in the title role. In 1944, Nelson appeared in a spiritless production of *Knickerbocker Holiday*, and in 1946 scored a minor triumph by singing the three voices of Willie the Whale in Walt Disney's imaginative *Make Mine Music*. By 1947, he was reduced to starring in a low-budget Republic musical horse opera, *Northwest Outpost*. Ilona Massey, his one-time MGM co-star, whose career was also on the skids, played opposite him. It was his last screen appearance.

After *Cairo*, Jeanette left films for a while and devoted herself to her concert career and her husband. During World War II, Gene joined the Air Force and emerged a captain. He later became a colonel

AFTERMATH

in the reserves. Jeanette meanwhile kept very busy in Army Emergency Relief shows, USO tours, radio appearances, and recitals. In February, 1943, the story got around that she was to make her long-awaited debut at the Metropolitan Opera House in Gounod's *Romeo et Juliette*. The trouble was, the management at the Met knew nothing about it. Later that same year, however, she appeared in her very first complete opera in Montreal. She was Juliette in the Gounod opera, opposite tenor Armand Tokatyan as Romeo. Featured in the supporting cast was the renowned bass Ezio Pinza. Wilfred Pelletier, the conductor, called her "a beautiful Juliet" and the local critics were unanimous in hailing her "auspicious debut," but she never did make it to the Met. Her tour of Canada and the United States in this production was extremely successful.

In 1944, she appeared for the first time as Marguerite in Gounod's *Faust*, and again received favorable notices in Chicago and other major cities. That same year, she was lured back to films for three brief sequences in a Universal all-star revue, *Follow the Boys*. She sang "I'll See You in My Dreams" and "Beyond the Blue Horizon" as charmingly as ever.

Her biggest on-stage triumph

CAIRO (1942). With Robert Young

CAIRO (1942). With Robert Young and Ethel Waters (at left)

FOLLOW THE BOYS (1944). With Ralph Gardner and Charles Brown

THREE DARING DAUGHTERS (1948). With Jose Iturbi

THREE DARING DAUGHTERS (1948). With Ann E. Todd, Jose Iturbi, Jane Powell, and Mary Eleanor Donahue

came in 1945, when her program of arias, popular tunes, and melodies associated with her movies drew a record crowd to the Hollywood Bowl.

Jeanette returned to MGM for *Three Daring Daughters* in 1947. Released early in 1948, this Joseph Pasternak entertainment featured Jeanette as a widow with three daughters, including Jane Powell, who object to her marriage to pianist José Iturbi, playing a pianist named José Iturbi. A viewer today tends to side with the kids.

Jeanette MacDonald appeared in only one more movie, *The Sun Comes Up*, released by MGM in 1949. She plays a widowed concert singer who loses her son but has her heart recaptured by an orphan boy (Claude Jarman, Jr. of *The Yearling*). The boy's faithful companion (and Jeanette's virtual co-star) was Lassie, who saves his master from an orphanage fire. *The New York Times* called the film "wholesome, inoffensive, banal."

In January, 1959, while watching her husband perform in a play in Washington, D.C., Jeanette collapsed and was rushed to a

THE SUN COMES UP (1949). With Claude Jarman, Jr. and Lassie

With husband Gene Raymond in 1950

hospital. Her appendix was removed, but she was never completely well again. Until her death in January, 1965, she was continually being treated for hepatitis and other ailments. Her husband, Gene, couldn't have been more concerned and attentive, but there was nothing he could do.

Jeanette's mother had died in 1947 at the age of seventy. Her co-star and friend, Nelson Eddy, died in March of 1967, after suffering a stroke while performing in a Palm Beach nightclub. Her oldest sister, Elsie, died in 1970. Blossom now resides at the Motion Picture County Home in Hollywood.

Gene Raymond and Allan Jones are both alive and well. Both have nothing but kind and loving words to say about the radiant redhead who, in her relatively brief film career, came to epitomize charm, grace, and beauty.

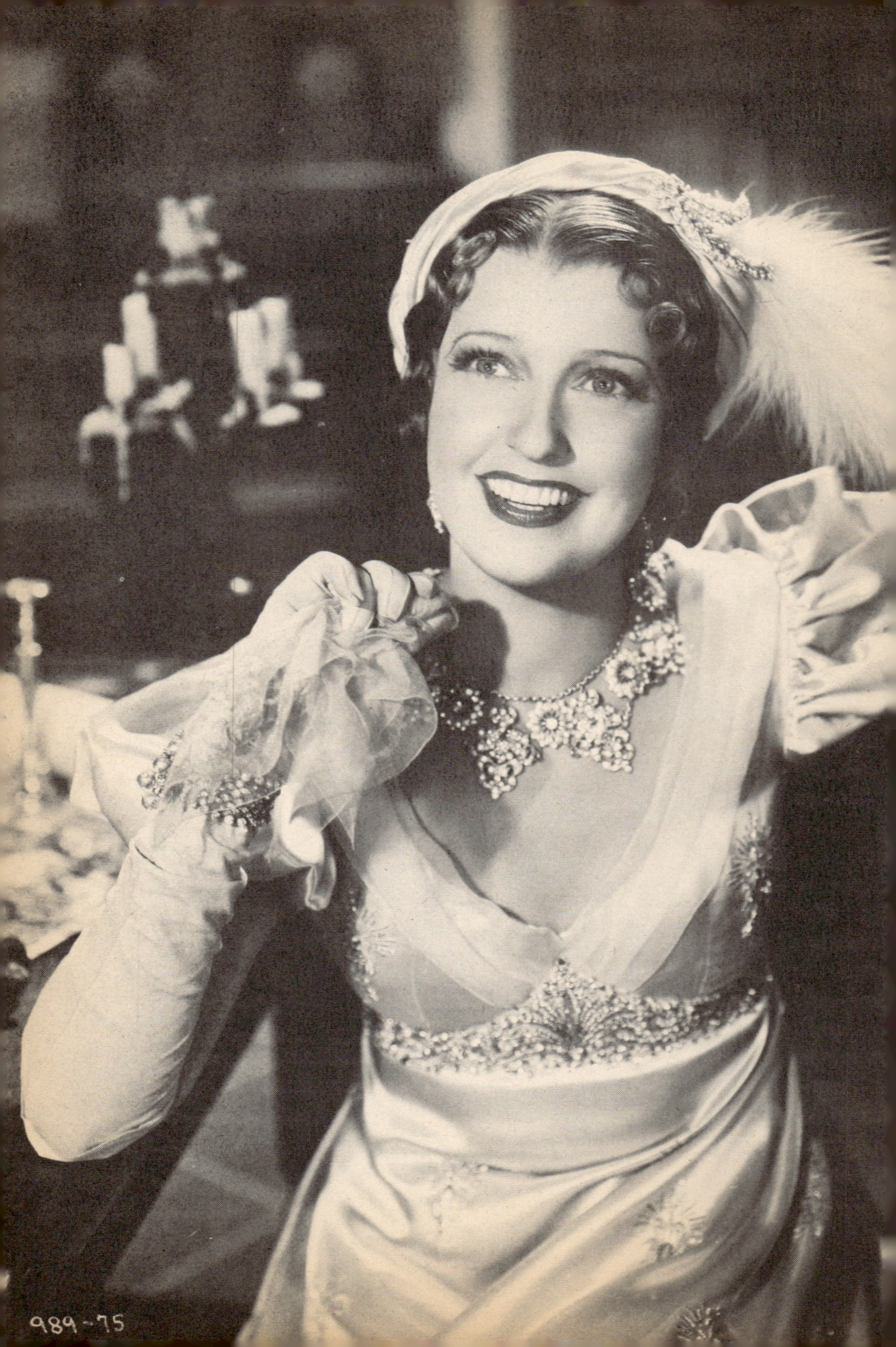

989-75

BIBLIOGRAPHY

Blum, Daniel (with Kobal, John). *A New Pictorial History of the Talkies*. G. P. Putnam's Sons, New York, 1973.

Knowles, Eleanor. *The Films of Jeanette MacDonald and Nelson Eddy*. A. S. Barnes and Co., Inc., Cranbury, New Jersey, 1975.

Kobal, John. *Gotta Sing Gotta Dance*. The Hamlyn Publishing Group Limited, London, New York, Sydney, Toronto, 1972.

McVay, Douglas. *The Musical Film*. A. Zwemmer Limited, London, A. S. Barnes & Co., New York, 1967.

Moore, Grace. *You're Only Human Once*. Latimer House, London, 1947.

New York Times Film Reviews, The: 1913-1968, Vols. 4, 5. The New York Times and Arno Press, New York, 1970.

Parish, James Robert. *The Jeanette MacDonald Story*. Mason/Charter, New York, 1976.

Roth, Lillian with Mike Connolly and Gerald Frank. *I'll Cry Tomorrow*. Frederick Fell, New York, 1954.

Stern, Lee Edward. *The Movie Musical*. Pyramid Publications, New York, 1974.

Taylor, John Russell and Jackson, Arthur. *The Hollywood Musical*. McGraw-Hill Book Company, New York, 1971.

Weinberg, Herman G. *The Lubitsch Touch*. E. P. Dutton, New York, 1968.

THE FILMS OF JEANETTE MacDONALD

The director's name follows the release date. A (c) *following the release date indicates that the film is in color.* Sp *indicates Screenplay.* MS *indicates Musical Score (composer and lyricist), and* b/o *indicates based on.*

1. THE LOVE PARADE. Paramount, 1929. *Ernst Lubitsch*. Sp: Guy Bolton, b/o *The Prince Consort*, play by Leon Xanrof and Jules Chancel. MS: Victor Schertzinger, Clifford Grey. Cast: Maurice Chevalier, Lupino Lane, Lillian Roth, Lionel Belmore, Virginia Bruce.

2. THE VAGABOND KING. Paramount, 1930. *Ludwig Berger*. Sp: Herman J. Mankiewicz, b/o novel *If I Were King*, by Justin Huntly McCarthy and operetta *The Vagabond King* by Rudolf Friml, William H. Post, and Brian Hooker. MS: Rudolf Friml, Brian Hooker, others. Cast: Dennis King, O.P. Heggie, Lillian Roth, Warner Oland. In "two-color Technicolor." Remade in 1938 as *If I Were King* (without music) and in 1956.

3. MONTE CARLO. Paramount, 1930. *Ernst Lubitsch*. Sp: Ernest Vadja, b/o story by Hans Mueller and an episode from the novel *Monsieur Beaucaire* by Booth Tarkington. MS: Richard Whiting and W. Franke Harling, Leo Robin. Cast: Jack Buchanan, ZaSu Pitts, Tyler Brooke, Claude Allister.

4. PARAMOUNT ON PARADE. Paramount, 1930. *Various directors*. Sp and MS: Various writers and composers. Cast: Maurice Chevalier, Richard Arlen, Jean Arthur, Clara Bow, Clive Brook, Gary Cooper, Fredric March, Dennis King, Jack Oakie, many other Paramount players. Some sequences in color.

5. LET'S GO NATIVE. Paramount-Public Corp., 1930. *Leo McCarey*. Sp: George Marion Jr. and Percy Heath. MS: Richard A. Whiting, George Marion Jr. Cast: Jack Oakie, James Hall, William Austin, Kay Francis, Richard "Skeets" Gallagher.

6. THE LOTTERY BRIDE. United Artists, 1930. *Paul Stein*. Sp: Horace Jackson, b/o story by Herbert Stothart. MS: Rudolf Friml, J. Keirn Brennan. Cast: John Garrick, Joe E. Brown, ZaSu Pitts.

7. OH, FOR A MAN, Fox, 1930. *Hamilton MacFadden*. Sp: Philip Klein, b/o story by Mary T. Watkins. Cast: Reginald Denny, Warren Hymer, Marjorie White, Alison Skipworth, Bela Lugosi.

8. DON'T BET ON WOMEN. Fox, 1931. *William K. Howard*. Sp: Lynn Starling and Leon Gordon, b/o story by William Anthony McGuire. Cast: Edmund Lowe, Roland Young, J. M. Kerrigan, Una Merkel, Louise Beavers.

9. ANNABELLE'S AFFAIRS. Fox, 1931. *Alfred L. Werker*. Sp: Leon Gordon, b/o *Good Gracious Annabelle*, play by Clare Kummer. Cast: Victor McLaglen, Roland Young, Sam Hardy, Louise Beavers.

10. ONE HOUR WITH YOU. Paramount, 1932. *Ernst Lubitsch and George Cukor*. Sp: Samson Raphaelson, b/o *Only a Dream*, play by Lothar Schmidt. MS: Oscar Straus and Richard A. White, Leo Robin. Cast: Maurice Chevalier, Genevieve Tobin, Charlie Ruggles, Roland Young.

11. LOVE ME TONIGHT. Paramount, 1932. *Rouben Mamoulian*. Sp: Samuel Hoffenstein, Waldemar Young, and George Marion Jr., b/o story by Leopold Marchand and Paul Arment. MS: Richard Rodgers, Lorenz Hart. Cast: Maurice Chevalier, Charlie Ruggles, Charles Butterworth, Myrna Loy, C. Aubrey Smith, Elizabeth Patterson.

12. THE CAT AND THE FIDDLE. MGM, 1934. *William K. Howard*. Sp: Samuel and Bella Spewack, b/o operetta by Jerome Kern and Otto Harbach. MS: Jerome Kern, Otto Harbach. Cast: Ramon Novarro, Frank Morgan, Charles Butterworth, Jean Hersholt, Vivienne Segal.

13. THE MERRY WIDOW. MGM, 1934. *Ernst Lubitsch*. Sp: Samson Raphaelson and Ernest Vajda, b/o operetta by Franz Lehar, Victor Leon, and Leo Stein. MS: Franz Lehar, Lorenz Hart and Gus Kahn. Cast: Maurice Chevalier, Edward Everett Horton, Una Merkel, George Barbier, Stanley Holloway, Akim Tamiroff. Also filmed in 1913, 1925 and 1952.

14. NAUGHTY MARIETTA. MGM, 1935. *W. S. Van Dyke II*. Sp: John Lee Mahin, Frances Goodrich and Albert Hackett, b/o operetta by Rida Johnson Young. MS: Victor Herbert. Cast: Nelson Eddy, Frank Morgan, Elsa Lanchester, Douglass Dumbrille, Akim Tamiroff, Harold Huber.

15. ROSE MARIE. MGM, 1936. *W. S. Van Dyke II*. Sp: Frances Goodrich, Albert Hackett, Alice Duer Miller, b/o musical by Rudolf Friml, Otto Harbach, and Oscar Hammerstein II. MS: Rudolf Friml and Herbert Stothart. Cast: Nelson Eddy, James Stewart, Reginald Owen, Una O'Connor, Alan Mowbray. Also filmed in 1928 and 1954.

16. SAN FRANCISCO. MGM, 1936. *W. S. Van Dyke II*. Sp: Anita Loos, b/o story by Robert Hopkins. Cast: Clark Gable, Spencer Tracy, Jack Holt, Harold Huber, Al Shean, Jessie Ralph.

17. MAYTIME. MGM, 1937. *Robert Z. Leonard*. Sp: Noel Langley, b/o operetta by Rida Johnson Young. MS: Sigmund Romberg and others, with special lyrics by Bob Wright and Chet Forrest. Cast: Nelson Eddy, John Barrymore, Herman Bing, Tom Brown, Lynne Carver.

18. THE FIREFLY. MGM, 1937. *Robert Z. Leonard*. Sp: Frances Goodrich, Albert Hackett, Ogden Nash, b/o operetta by Otto Harbach. MS: Rudolf Friml, Otto Harbach. Cast: Allan Jones, Warren William, Douglass Dumbrille, Billy Gilbert, Henry Daniell, George Zucco.

19. THE GIRL OF THE GOLDEN WEST. MGM, 1938. *Robert Z. Leonard*. Sp: Isabel Dawn and Boyce DeGaw, b/o play by David Belasco. MS: Sigmund Romberg, Gus Kahn. Cast: Nelson Eddy, Walter Pidgeon, Buddy Ebsen, Leo Carrillo, H. B. Warner. Also filmed in 1923 and 1930.

20. SWEETHEARTS. MGM, 1939 (c). *W. S. Van Dyke II*. Sp: Dorothy Parker and Alan Campbell, b/o operetta by Fred DeGresac, Harry B. Smith, and Robert B. Smith. MS: Victor Herbert, new lyrics by Bob Wright and Chet Forrest. Cast: Nelson Eddy, Frank Morgan, Ray Bolger, Mischa Auer, Reginald Gardiner.

21. BROADWAY SERENADE. MGM, 1939. *Robert Z. Leonard*. Sp: Charles Lederer, b/o original screen story by Lew Lipton, John Taintor Foote, and Hans Kraly. MS: Various composers and lyricists. Cast: Lew Ayres, Ian Hunter, Frank Morgan, Rita Johnson, Virginia Grey, Al Shean.

22. NEW MOON. MGM, 1940. *Robert Z. Leonard*. Sp: Jacques Deval and Robert Arthur, b/o operetta by Oscar Hammerstein II, Frank Mandel and Laurence Schwag. MS: Sigmund Romberg, Oscar Hammerstein II. Cast: Nelson Eddy, Mary Boland, George Zucco, H. B. Warner, Buster Keaton. Also filmed in 1930.

23. BITTER SWEET. MGM, 1940 (c). *W. S. Van Dyke II*. Sp: Lesser Samuels, b/o musical play by Noël Coward. MS: Noël Coward. Cast: Nelson Eddy, Ian Hunter, George Sanders, Felix Bressart, Curt Bois, Herman Bing. Also filmed in 1933.

24. SMILIN' THROUGH. MGM, 1941 (c). *Frank Borzage*. Sp: Donald Ogden Stewart and John Balderston, b/o play by Jane Cowl and Jane Murfin. MS: Various composers and lyricists. Cast: Brian Aherne, Gene Raymond, Ian Hunter, Frances Robinson. Also filmed in 1922 and 1932.

25. I MARRIED AN ANGEL. MGM, 1942. *W. S. Van Dyke II*. Sp: Anita Loos, b/o play by Vaszary Janos. MS: Richard Rodgers, Lorenz Hart. Cast: Nelson Eddy, Binnie Barnes, Edward Everett Horton, Reginald Owen, Douglass Dumbrille, Leonid Kinskey.

26. CAIRO. MGM, 1942. *W. S. Van Dyke II*. Sp: John McClain, b/o idea by Ladislas Fodor. Cast: Robert Young, Ethel Waters, Reginald Owen, Mona Barrie, Lionel Atwill.

27. FOLLOW THE BOYS. Universal, 1944. *Eddie Sutherland*. Sp: Lou Breslow and Gertrude Purcell. MS: Various composers and lyricists. Cast: George Raft, Vera Zorina, Charles Grapewin, Charles Butterworth, many "guest stars" including Orson Welles, Marlene Dietrich, Dinah Shore, Sophie Tucker.

28. THREE DARING DAUGHTERS. MGM, 1948 (c). *Fred Wilcox*. Sp: Albert Mannheimer, Frederick Kohner, Sonya Levien, and John Meehan. Cast: José Iturbi, Jane Powell, Ann E. Todd, Mary Eleanor Donahue, Edward Arnold, Harry Davenport.

29. THE SUN COMES UP. MGM, 1949 (c). *Richard Thorpe*. Sp: William Ludwig and Margaret Fitts, b/o *Saturday Evening Post* story by Marjorie Kinnan Rawlings. Cast: Lloyd Nolan, Lassie, Claude Jarman Jr., Percy Kilbride, Lewis Stone, Margaret Hamilton.

INDEX

Adrian, 23
Aherne, Brian, 130
Aida, 85
Allister, Claude, 41
Angela, 26
Annabelle's Affairs, 44, 46
Applause, 50
Arlen, Richard, 41
Arliss, George, 36
Arthur, Jean, 41
Astaire, Fred, 11, 54, 85
Atkinson, Brooks, 26
Ayres, Lew, 117, 125

Balalaika, 125
Barbier, George, 69
Barrymore, John, 11, 114, 117
Belasco, David, 121
Ben-Hur, 59
Benny, Jack, 53
Bergen, Edgar, 85
Berger, Ludwig, 36
Berkeley, Busby, 54
Big Pond, The, 36
Bing, Herman, 127
Bitter Sweet, 126-127
Blyth, Ann, 99
Bodenheim, Maxwell, 23
Boehnel, William, 112
Bogart, Humphrey, 26, 30
Boland, Mary, 26
Bolger, Ray, 125
Bolton, Guy, 35
Boom! Boom!, 29
Borzage, Frank, 127
Brady, Alice, 85
Brewster's Millions, 26
Brice, Fanny, 16
Broadway Serenade, 125
Broadway to Hollywood, 85
Brown, Joe E., 43
Brown, Tom, 114
Bubblin' Over, 26
Buchanan, Jack, 41, 48
Burnett, Carol, 11
Bushman, Francis X., 59
Butterworth, Charles, 53, 61, 86

Cagney, James, 30
Cairo, 139
Campbell, Alan, 125
Cantor, Eddie, 53
Carousel, 54
Carver, Lynne, 114
Cat and the Fiddle, The, 59, 61
Chevalier, Maurice, 11, 12, 29, 30, 32, 35, 36, 41, 48, 49, 50, 53, 54, 66, 76, 79, 137
Chocolate Soldier, The, 130
Colbert, Claudette, 30, 39
Colman, Ronald, 36
Cooper, Gary, 41
Coward, Noël, 41, 126
Cradle-Snatchers, The, 26
Crawford, Joan, 69, 85, 117
Crowther, Bosley, 125, 126
Cuban Love Song, 80
Cukor, George, 48, 49

Dancing Lady, 85
de Schauensee, Max, 82
Demi-Tasse Revue, The, 17, 21, 62
Denny, Reginald, 44
Dix, Richard, 26, 29
Dr. Jekyll and Mr. Hyde, 50
Dolly, Rosie, 90
Don't Bet on Women, 44, 59
Duchess of Delmonico's, The, 56
Dumbrille, Douglass, 86
Durante, Jimmy, 80, 86

Eddy, Nelson, 11, 12, 56, 76, 80, 82, 85, 86, 90, 94, 96, 113, 114, 117, 118, 121, 125, 126, 130, 136, 139, 145
Eisenhower, Dwight D., 16

Fantastic Fricassee, 23
Ferguson, Helen, 80
Firefly, The, 12, 90, 117, 119, 121, 126
Follow the Boys, 139
Forrest, Chet, 121, 136
Frazee, H.H., 26
Friml, Rudolf, 36, 43, 118, 121

Gable, Clark, 11, 85, 90, 99, 111, 112

155

Gallagher, Skeets, 41
Garrick, John, 43
Gershwin, George, 26
Gershwin, Ira, 26
Gigi, 79
Girl of the Golden West, The, 121-125
Goldwater, Barry, 16
Good Gracious, Annabelle, 46
Goodrich, Francis, 93
Goulding, Edmund, 113
Gray, Gilda, 95
Greenstreet, Sydney, 23
Guion, Raymond (see Gene Raymond)

Hackett, Albert, 93
Hall, Mordaunt, 36
Hammerstein, Oscar, 54
Harbach, Otto, 59
Hart, Lorenz, 53, 54, 56, 66, 86, 130
Hart, Moss, 56
Hecht, Ben, 23
Herbert, Victor, 80, 125
Hersholt, Jean, 61
Hoag, Mitzi, 23
Holt, Jack, 108
Hopkins, Robert, 99
Horton, Edward Everett, 69, 71
Howard, William K., 44, 59
Hunter, Ian, 127

I Married An Angel, 56, 130, 136, 139
If I Were King, 36
Il Pagliacci, 85
Indian Love Call (Rose Marie), 96
Irene, 21

Jarman, Claude, Jr., 143
Jazz Singer, The, 30
Jolson, Al, 53, 108
Jones, Allan, 11, 12, 80, 90, 93, 117, 118, 121, 138, 145

Kahn, Gus, 66
Keel, Howard, 99
Kern, Jerome, 21, 59
King, Dennis, 36, 39, 93
Knickerbocker Holiday, 139
Koverman, Ida, 85
Kummer, Clare, 44

Lanchester, Elsa, 86
Lane, Lupino, 32
Lassie, 143

Lehar, Franz, 62, 66
Lehman, Lotte, 85
Leon, Victor, 66
Leonard, Robert Z., 118, 121, 125, 126
Let Freedom Ring, 125
Let's Go Native, 41, 43
Lindbergh, Charles, 47
Lippe, Edouard, 86
Littlefield, Caroline, 17
Littlefield, James B., 17
Lloyd, Harold, 117
Loos, Anita, 130
Lottery Bride, The, 43, 44
Love Me Tonight, 50, 53-54
Love Parade, The, 29, 30, 32-36, 41, 44, 46
Lowe, Edmund, 44
Loy, Myrna, 53, 80
Lubitsch, Ernst, 11, 29, 30, 32, 35, 41, 44, 48, 49, 54, 61, 66, 69, 76, 79
Lukas, Paul, 113
Lupino, Ida, 35

MacDonald, Anna Wright (mother), 17, 20, 30, 61, 145
MacDonald, Daniel (father), 17, 20
MacDonald, Edith Blossom (sister) (Marie Blake), 16, 20, 21, 26, 61, 117, 145
MacDonald, Elsie (sister), 17, 117, 145
McCarey, Leo, 41, 43
McCormack, John, 16
McLaglen, Victor, 46
Magic Ring, The, 23
Make Mine Music, 139
Mamoulian, Rouben, 50, 53, 54
Man I Killed, The, 49
Mannequin, 117
March, Fredric, 30, 41, 50
Marchand, Leopold, 53
Marriage Circle, The, 48
Marriage Tax, The, 82
Marshall, Herbert, 56
Martin, Mildred, 39, 54
Marx Brothers, The, 43
Massey, Ilona, 121, 125, 139
Mayer, Louis B., 12, 54, 56, 61, 80, 85, 99, 113, 114, 117, 121, 125, 137
Maytime, 12, 90, 99, 113-115, 117, 121, 137
Merkel, Una, 44, 70, 93
Merry Widow, The, 12, 32, 62, 66, 69-71, 76, 79, 80, 114
Meyer, Richard, 26
Miller, Alice Duer, 93
Miller, Marilyn, 16

Mizner, Wilson, 99
Monte Carlo, 41, 47
Moore, Grace, 16, 66, 69, 76, 93
Morgan, Frank, 61, 85, 86, 113
Morgan, Helen, 50
Mowbray, Alan, 93
Mutiny on the Bounty, 99

Naughty Marietta, 80, 85, 86, 90, 93, 96, 126, 138
New Moon, 125-126
Night Boat, The, 21
Niven, David, 93
No, No, Nanette, 26
Nolan, Lloyd, 16
Northwest Outpost, 139
Novarro, Ramon, 59, 61
Nugent, Frank S., 113

Oakie, Jack, 41
Oh, For a Man, 44, 93
Oklahoma!, 54
Oland, Warner, 36
Oliver, Edna May, 26
One Hour With You, 48-49
One Night of Love, 16, 66
Owen, Reginald, 93

Paramount on Parade, 41
Parker, Dorothy, 125
Pasternak, Joseph, 143
Pelletier, Wilfred, 139
Phantom of the Opera, The, 139
Pidgeon, Walter, 121
Pinza, Ezio, 139
Pitts, ZaSu, 43
Pons, Lily, 30, 69
Porgy and Bess, 54
Porter, Cole, 121
Potters, The, 26
Powell, Eleanor, 121
Powell, Jane, 143
Powell, William, 41, 80

Rains, Claude, 139
Rasch, Albertina, 21
Rathbone, Basil, 117
Raymond, Gene, 12, 16, 26, 90, 117, 127, 130, 139, 145
Regas, George, 94
Ritchie, Robert, 12, 30, 36, 41, 44, 48, 54, 56, 80
Robin, Leo, 26

Robinson, Edward G., 30
Rock, Warren, 117
Rodgers, Richard, 53, 54, 56, 86, 130
Rogers, Ginger, 11, 54
Romberg, Sigmund, 99, 114, 125
Rosalie, 121
Rose Marie, 12, 44, 90-96, 114, 121, 126, 137
Roth, Lillian, 35, 36

Samuels, Lesser, 126
San Francisco, 12, 90, 99-105, 108, 111-113, 118
Sanders, George, 127
Schertzinger, Victor, 35
Schulberg, B.P., 49
Segal, Vivienne, 61, 69
Shean, Al, 108
Shearer, Norma, 127
Smilin' Through, 127, 130
Smith, C. Aubrey, 53
Stanwyck, Barbara, 30
Stein, Leo, 66
Stevens, Risë, 130
Stewart, James, 90, 96
Stromberg, Hunt, 136
Student Tour, 86
Sullivan, Ed, 86
Sun Comes Up, The, 143
Sunny Days, 26
Sweethearts, 125

Tamiroff, Akim, 86
Tangerine, 23
Tarzan, The Ape Man, 80
Temple, Shirley, 56
Thalberg, Irving, 54, 56, 66, 69, 99
Thin Man, The, 80
Three Daring Daughters, 143
Tibbett, Lawrence, 30, 80
Tip Toes, 26
Tokatyan, Armand, 139
Tracy, Spencer, 11, 90, 99, 107, 112, 117
Tucker, Sophie, 17

Vagabond King, The, 36, 39
Van Dyke, W.S. II, 80, 86, 90, 99, 108, 125, 126, 139
Velez, Lupe, 80
von Stroheim, Erich, 66

Waters, Ethel, 139
Watts, Richard, 35

Wayburn, Ned, 17
White, Al, 17
Wilson, Dooley, 139
Worth, Eleanor, 21
Wright, Bob, 121, 136

Yearling, The, 143

Yes, Yes, Yvette, 26
Young, Loretta, 90
Young, Robert, 139
Young, Roland, 44, 46

Zoo in Budapest, 90
Zukor, Adolph, 50

ABOUT THE AUTHOR
Lee Edward Stern is a public relations executive, writer, and radio commentator on the arts. He has written on many subjects for many publications and is the author of *The Movie Musical*.

ABOUT THE EDITOR
Ted Sennett is the author of *Warner Brothers Presents*, a tribute to the great Warner films of the thirties and forties, and of *Lunatics and Lovers*, on the long-vanished but well-remembered "screwball" movie comedies of the past. He is also editor of *The Movie Buff's Book*, *The Old-Time Radio Book*, and *The Movie Buff's Book: 2*.